T 41   P9-CFL-312

ᵀᴴᴱ**new** biology

Gene Therapy

Revised Edition

ᴛʜᴇ **new** biology

Gene Therapy

Treatments and Cures for Genetic Diseases
Revised Edition

JOSEPH PANNO, PH.D.

☑️ Facts On File

An imprint of Infobase Publishing

GENE THERAPY: Treatments and Cures for Genetic Diseases, Revised Edition

Copyright © 2011, 2005 by Joseph Panno, Ph.D.

Facts On File, Inc.
An imprint of Infobase Publishing
132 West 31st Street
New York NY 10001

Library of Congress Cataloging-in-Publication Data

Panno, Joseph.
    Gene therapy : treatments and cures for genetic diseases / Joseph Panno.—Rev. ed.
        p. cm.—(The new biology)
    Includes bibliographical references and index.
    ISBN 978-0-8160-6850-0
    1. Gene therapy. I. Title
    RB155.8.P36 2011
    615.8'95—dc22   2009045854

Facts On File books are available at special discounts when purchased in bulk quantities for businesses, associations, institutions, or sales promotions. Please call our Special Sales Department in New York at (212) 967-8800 or (800) 322-8755.

You can find Facts On File on the World Wide Web at http://www.factsonfile.com

Text design by Erik Lindstrom
Composition by Hermitage Publishing Services
Illustrations by the author
Photo research by Diane K. French
Cover printed by Bang Printing, Brainerd, Minn.
Book printed and bound by Bang Printing, Brainerd, Minn.
Date printed: September 2010
Printed in the United States of America

10 9 8 7 6 5 4 3 2 1

This book is printed on acid-free paper.

Contents

Preface

When the first edition of this set was being written, the new biology was just beginning to come into its potential and to experience some of its first failures. Dolly the sheep was alive and well and had just celebrated her fifth birthday. Stem cell researchers, working 12-hour days, were giddy with the prospect of curing every disease known to humankind, but were frustrated by inconsistent results and the limited availability of human embryonic stem cells. Gene therapists, still reeling from the disastrous Gelsinger trial of 1998, were busy trying to figure out what had gone wrong and how to improve the safety of a procedure that many believed would revolutionize medical science. And cancer researchers, while experiencing many successes, hit their own speed bump when a major survey showed only modest improvements in the prognosis for all of the deadliest cancers.

During the 1970s, when the new biology was born, recombinant technology served to reenergize the sagging discipline that biology had become. This same level of excitement reappeared in the 1990s with the emergence of gene therapy, the cloning of Dolly the sheep, and the successful cultivation of stem cells. Recently, great excitement has come with the completion of the human genome project and the genome sequencing of more than 100 animal and plant species. Careful analysis of these genomes has spawned a new branch of biological research known as comparative genomics. The information that scientists can now extract from animal genomes is expected to improve all other branches of biological science. Not to be outdone, stem cell researchers have found a way to produce embryo-like stem cells from ordinary skin cells. This achievement not only marks the end of the great stem cell debate, but it also provides an immensely powerful procedure, known as cellular dedifferentiation, for studying and manipulating the very essence of a cell. This procedure will become a crucial weapon in the fight against cancer and many other diseases.

The new biology, like our expanding universe, has been growing and spreading at an astonishing rate. The amount of information that is now available on these topics is of astronomical proportions. Thus, the problem of deciding what to leave out has become as difficult as the decision of what to include. The guiding principle in writing this set has always been to provide a thorough overview of the topics without overwhelming the reader with a mountain of facts and figures. To be sure, this set contains many facts and figures, but these have been carefully chosen to illustrate only the essential principles.

This edition, in keeping with the expansion of the biological disciplines, has grown to accommodate new material and new areas of research. Four new books have been added that focus on areas of biological research that are reaping the benefits of genome science and modern research technologies. Thus, the New Biology set now consists of the following 10 volumes:

1. *Aging*, Revised Edition
2. *Animal Cloning*, Revised Edition
3. *Cancer*, Revised Edition
4. *The Cell*, Revised Edition
5. *Gene Therapy*, Revised Edition
6. *Stem Cell Research*, Revised Edition
7. *Genome Research*
8. *The Immune System*
9. *Modern Medicine*
10. *Viruses*

Many new chapters have been added to each of the original six volumes, and the remaining chapters have been extensively revised and updated. The number of figures and photos in each book has increased significantly, and all are now rendered in full color. The new volumes, following the same format as the originals, greatly expand the scope of the New Biology set and serve to emphasize the fact that these technologies are not just about finding cures for diseases but are helping scientists understand a wide range of biological processes. Even a partial list of these revelations is impressive: detailed information on every gene and every protein that is needed to build a human being; eventual identification of all cancer genes, stem cell–specific genes, and longevity genes; mapping of safe chromosomal insertion sites for gene therapy; and the identification of genes that control the growth of the human brain, the development of speech, and the maintenance of mental stability. In a stunning achievement, genome researchers have been able to trace the exact route our human ancestors used to emigrate from Africa nearly 65,000 years ago and even to estimate the number of individuals who made up the original group.

In addition to the accelerating pace of discovery, the new biology has made great strides in resolving past mistakes and failures. The Gelsinger trial was a dismal failure that killed a young man in the prime of his life, but gene therapy trials in the next 10 years will be astonishing, both for their success and for their safety. For the past 50 years, cancer researchers have been caught in a desperate struggle as they tried to control the growth and spread of deadly tumors, but many scientists are now confident that cancer will be eliminated by 2020. Viruses, such as HIV or the flu, are resourceful and often deadly adversaries, but genome researchers are about to put the fight on more rational grounds as detailed information is obtained about viral genes, viral life cycles, and viruses' uncanny ability to evade or cripple the human immune system.

These struggles and more are covered in this edition of the New Biology set. I hope the discourse will serve to illustrate both the power of science and the near superhuman effort that has gone into the creation and validation of these technologies.

Acknowledgments

I would first like to thank the legions of science graduate students and postdoctoral fellows who have made the new biology a practical reality. They are the unsung heroes of this discipline. The clarity and accuracy of the initial manuscript for this book was much improved by reviews and comments from Diana Dowsley, Michael Panno, Rebecca Lapres, and later by Frank K. Darmstadt, executive editor, and the rest of the Facts On File staff. I am also indebted to Diane K. French and Elizabeth Oakes for their help in securing photographs for the New Biology set. Finally, as always, I would like to thank my wife and daughter for keeping the ship on an even keel.

Introduction

When we get sick it often is due to invading microbes that destroy or damage cells and organs in our body. Cholera, smallpox, measles, diphtheria, AIDS, and the common cold are all examples of what we call infectious diseases. If we catch any of these diseases, our physician may prescribe a drug that will, in some cases, remove the microbe from our bodies, thus curing the disease.

Unfortunately, most of the diseases that we fall prey to are not of the infectious kind. There are no microbes to fight, no drugs to apply. Instead, we are faced with a far more difficult problem, for this type of disease is an ailment of our genes. Since the 1990s, scientists have identified several thousand gene mutations that are known to be responsible for diseases such as cancer, cystic fibrosis, hemophilia, and Parkinson's disease. Gene therapy attempts to cure these diseases by replacing or supplementing the gene that is causing the problem.

Although there are thousands of genetic defects that could, in principle, be treated with gene therapy, only a small percentage are considered practical candidates for this type of treatment. Diseases that qualify for gene therapy are debilitating disorders that affect more than 1 percent of the population, the conventional treatments for which are ineffective, costly, or difficult to administer. Many people opt for gene therapy simply because it is their best chance for a normal life, even if they are not completely cured. Gene therapy is potentially dangerous, and thus special attention must be paid to the selection process. All clinical trials are carefully screened and monitored by government granting agencies. For example, trials conducted in the United States are regulated by the Food and Drug Administration (FDA) and the National Institutes of Health (NIH), while trials in the United Kingdom are controlled by the Gene Therapy Advisory Committee, established by the Department of Health.

The first gene therapy trial, conducted in 1991, was designed to treat an immune system disorder known as adenosine deaminase (ADA) deficiency. ADA weakens the immune response so that individuals suffering from this disorder are unable to fight off even mild infections. There were only two patients in that trial, one of whom showed a modest recovery while the second patient, a young girl named Ashi DeSilva, showed a dramatic improvement. This trial proved to the research community that gene therapy could work. Many other gene therapy trials were launched throughout the 1990s, but none of them lived up to expectations. Indeed, a trial conducted at the University of Pennsylvania in 1998 ended in disaster when one of the patients, a young man named Jesse Gelsinger, died as a direct result of the treatment. The consequences of this trial were profound as they affected not only gene therapy but also all experimental therapies that involve human subjects. Critics at the time pointed out that gene therapy should not be called a therapy at all, but an experimental procedure, a status that it retains to this day.

Since the birth of recombinant DNA technology in the early 1970s, scientists have dreamed of using their new tool kit to cure genetic diseases, and now it appears that dream may come true. But the fulfillment of that dream is producing a therapy that is extremely hazardous and surprisingly difficult to apply. The complicating element of the therapy is reliance on a virus to carry the therapeutic gene into the patient's cells. Generally, the virus, known as a vector or gene vehicle, is injected into the bloodstream where it comes into contact with cells of the immune system. The immune system destroys most of the vector particles before they can enter the appropriate cells, thus abolishing much of the therapeutic effect. When the vector gains access to some of the cells, the immune system treats this as any other infection and tries to kill the cells harboring the vector. The immune system attack on the infected cells has two consequences: The immune system kills the cells containing the vector, thus further minimizing any therapeutic effect or, if the number of cells harboring the vector is very high, the immune system will damage or destroy whole organs in an attempt to rid the body of the vector, with potentially fatal consequences for the patient. Despite these very substantial problems, the number of disorders being treated with gene therapy has increased from a few in 1990 to more than 900 in 2009. Of all the technologies provided by the new biology, gene therapy holds the promise of unlimited potential for curing disease and reversing the effects of age.

Gene Therapy, Revised Edition, one volume in the multivolume New Biology set, discusses the science behind gene therapy, as well as the ethical and legal issues associated with it. This edition contains updated and revised material throughout. Many new figures and photos have been added and all are now in color. In addition, most of the original figures were redrawn to enhance their clarity.

Two new chapters (1 and 9) have been added: Chapter 1 introduces genomic research, including genome sequencing projects, gene structure, and gene mutations. It provides all of the background information the reader needs to understand the material in the rest of the book. Chapter 9 is focused on a discussion of many recent gene therapy clinical trials, including a rationale for the trials and the methods being used. Although gene therapy has not yet been approved for routine medical use, the success of some of the clinical trials discussed in chapter 9 has inspired the new subtitle of this book. Chapter 2 (formerly chapter 1) has been expanded to include additional genetic diseases, including retinal dystrophy, a form of blindness that is now being treated with gene therapy in a Phase I clinical trial. The remaining chapters, dealing with virology, case studies, future prospects, and legal and ethical issues, have been updated whenever possible. The final chapter, as before, provides background material on cell biology, biotechnology, and other topics relevant to gene therapy. The cell biology and biotechnology primers have been extensively revised and condensed to improve the clarity of this important background information.

In the first edition, the future prospects of gene therapy were examined from the perspective of its one great success (Ashi DeSilva) and its greatest failure (Jesse Gelsinger). Despite the DeSilva trial, the death of Gelsinger threw a pall over the field that made scientists and the general public doubt the future of this therapy. But the advances of recent years, which include new vectors, new strategies, and the sequencing of the human genome, have reinvigorated the field. There is now a growing certainty within the science community that gene therapy will assume a central role in the fight against cancer, neurological disorders, and many other diseases.

The Human Genome

It is hard to pick up a newspaper these days without encountering some reference to the human genome. Biologists, all aglow over the completion of the Human Genome Project, wax lyrical about the endless discoveries that are possible now that the human genome has been sequenced. Not content with this sequence alone, research groups around the world are working long hours to sequence the genomes of many other organisms. In 2009, the list included more than 60 mammalian species, 54 invertebrates, and a large number of bacterial, fungal, protozoan, and viral species. Of special interest is the inclusion of the chimpanzee, gorilla, and orangutan, three of our closest primate relatives. The information obtained from this colossal undertaking is expected to revolutionize medical science and will surely help anthropologists unravel the many mysteries associated with human evolution.

But while the applications of genome research, or genomics, are discussed far and wide, the nature of the genome itself is often overlooked. In the world of architecture, a genome would be analogous to the blueprints for a house: Every window, every doorway, every room, and the location of every light fixture are carefully drawn out on large pieces of paper so the carpenters, electricians, and plumbers can build the house exactly as it was planned. With blueprints, nothing is left to chance. And if someone wants to build another house just like the original, or dozens of houses just like it, they have the blueprints to follow. In the cell's world, blueprints are called genes. A group of all the genes needed to build a cell or an animal or a plant is called a genome. In other words, the genome is an organism's complete set of building instructions, all encoded by DNA. The human genome consists of about 30,000 genes located on 23 pieces of DNA. Each piece of DNA is known as a chromosome, and every cell in a human body has 23 chromosomes from the mother and 23 from the father.

HISTORICAL BACKGROUND

The birth of a newborn child is usually followed by comparisons between the child's physical traits and those of his or her parents. The child may have the mother's nose, the father's eyes, and the grandmother's disposition. People have been aware of these inherited physical characteristics for thousands of years. Long before the advent of modern science, animal and plant breeders used a general knowledge of inheritance patterns to produce a great variety of horses, dogs, cats, and crops such as corn, rice, wheat, peanuts, and apples. Despite the success of these early breeders, careful analysis of inheritance patterns was not attempted until the 1860s when Gregor Mendel, an Austrian monk, began crossing pea plants that had well-defined traits. Mendel's experiments led him to conclude that many of the pea's traits were controlled by two distinct factors (now called genes), one coming from the father (or male plant) and the other from the mother.

Gregor Mendel (1822–84), Austrian monk and biologist. Mendel conducted experiments in a monastery in the 1860s with garden peas, working out the law of heredity based on "factors" (genes) that decide which characteristics are passed from parent to offspring. His work, documented in his monograph *Experiments with Plant Hybrids,* remained unnoticed until 1900. *(Science Source/Photo Researchers, Inc.)*

As exciting as Mendel's experiments were, next to nothing was known about the inheritance factors, and very few scientists took an interest in this topic. Even after the emergence of biochemistry, cell biology, and microbiology in the late 1800s and the discovery of important biochemical pathways in the 1930s, no one had identified the molecular nature of a gene. By the 1950s, biochemists had identified most of the molecules and macromolecules (chains of molecules) that are present in every cell, the two most abundant being the macromolecules DNA and protein. Many scientists believed that genes were made from protein because it was known to have a more complex structure than DNA. Other scientists argued that DNA was the likely candidate since it was the dominant macromolecule in the nucleus. The issue was resolved in 1952 when Martha Chase and Alfred Hershey proved that DNA, and not protein, is the genetic material of a cell. Their experiment depended on the fact that bacteria, like humans, are subject to viral infections. A virus that infects a bacterium is called a bacteriophage, or phage for short. Using the newly developed electron microscope, other scientists had been able to observe a phage attaching to a bacterial

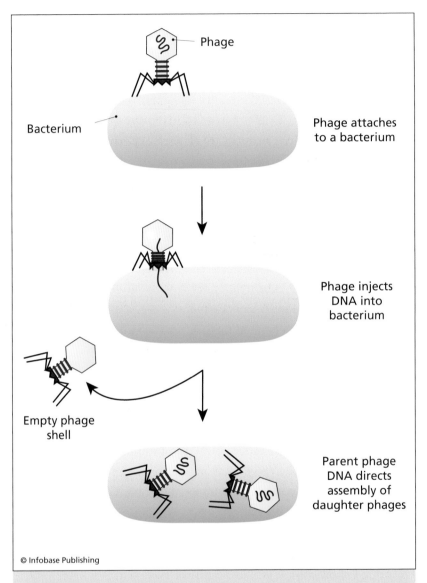

Phage

Bacterium

Phage attaches
to a bacterium

Phage injects
DNA into
bacterium

Empty phage
shell

Parent phage
DNA directs
assembly of
daughter phages

© Infobase Publishing

Identifying DNA as genetic material. By labeling the phage's DNA with an isotope of phosphorus and its protein with an isotope of sulfur, Martha Chase and Alfred Hershey were able to show that the phage always injects DNA into the host bacterium.

cell, after which the virus, acting like a tiny syringe, injected a long threadlike molecule into the bacterium. Within a few hours, phage particles could be seen forming inside the bacteria, after which the cells lysed, or burst open, releasing the newly made daughter phage to infect other bacteria. What did the parental phage inject into the bacteria: protein, DNA, or both? This is the question everyone wanted to answer. In a beautifully elegant experiment, Chase and Hershey showed that the phage always injects DNA, not protein, into the bacterium.

With the identity of the cell's genetic material firmly established, investigators turned their attention to learning more about DNA. In 1953, James Watson and Francis Crick, then working at the Cavendish Laboratory of Cambridge University, published a model for the structure of this macromolecule. DNA was shown to be a double helix, consisting of a linear sequence of four different nucleotides encoding the genetic information. In their paper, published in the journal *Nature,* Watson and Crick pointed out that the process of complementary nucleotide pairing provides a simple mechanism for gene duplication prior to cell division.

Mendel's experiments showed that some traits could be inherited together, whereas others were always inherited independently. Cytologists in the early 1900s were able to explain this difference by assuming that the inheritance factors, or genes, were associated with the newly discovered chromosomes that were observed to form during the cell cycle. (This cycle is discussed in chapter 10.) These studies showed that the two daughter cells received a random mix of paternal and maternal chromosomes. Thus, genes located on the same chromosome would be inherited together whereas those located on separate chromosomes would not.

These insights, along with the molecular model of DNA proposed by Watson and Crick, gave scientists a clear view of what is now known as the cell's genome: a collection of two or more

Discoverers of the structure of DNA. James Watson (1928–   ) at left and Francis Crick (1916–2004) are seen with their model of part of a DNA molecule in 1953. They met at the Cavendish Laboratory, Cambridge, in 1951. Their work on the structure of DNA was performed with knowledge of Chargaff's ratios of the bases in DNA and some access to the X-ray crystallography of Maurice Wilkins and Rosalind Franklin at King's College London. Combining all of this work led to the deduction that DNA exists as a double helix, thus to its structure. Crick, Watson, and Wilkins shared the 1962 Nobel Prize in physiology or medicine, Franklin having died of cancer in 1958. *(A. Barrington Brown/Photo Researchers, Inc.)*

chromosomes, each of which consists of a single molecule of DNA, upon which the genes are laid out in a sequential fashion. By the 1970s, scientists had worked out the complete genetic code that the cell uses to translate a gene sequence into a protein (see table on page 10). A crucial element in this process is the synthesis of a special kind of nucleic acid known as messenger ribonucleic acid (messenger RNA or mRNA), which serves as an intermediary between the DNA and the protein synthesizing machinery.

In 1976, the British biochemist Fred Sanger, then at the University of Cambridge, discovered a way to sequence DNA. Scientists

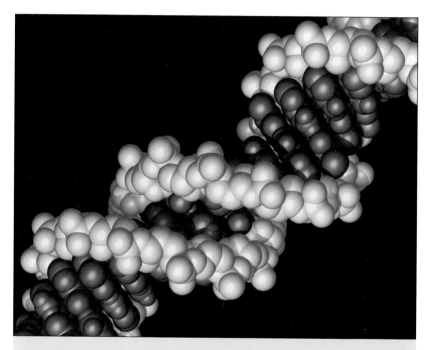

DNA molecule. A computer graphic representing a segment of the molecule deoxyribonucleic acid (DNA). This is the more common beta form of DNA where the spiral winds clockwise when viewed from above. DNA contains all the inherited instructions necessary to produce a living organism. Atoms are depicted as spheres. The DNA molecule is made of two strands of atoms (silver, bronze) twisted into a helical shape. Each strand consists of an outer sugar-phosphate backbone, from which nucleotide bases project. The bases are paired in a complementary fashion, and it is this base-pairing that forms the genetic code. *(K. Seddon and T. Evans/Photo Researchers, Inc.)*

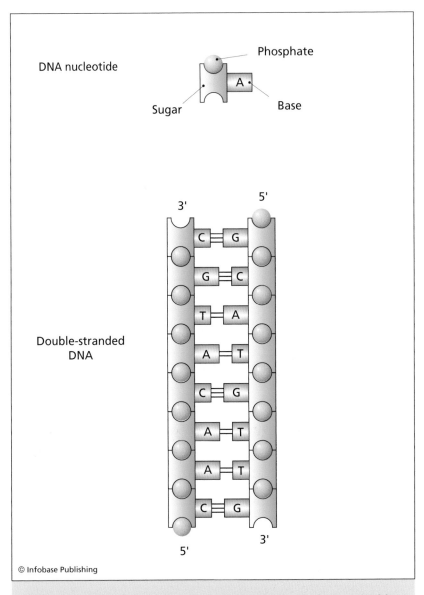

DNA structure. Nucleotides are linked together to form a double-stranded molecule. The bases are held together with double or triple bonds, and the two strands are antiparallel. This section of DNA is shown flat for clarity. In reality, the two strands twist around each other to form a double helix.

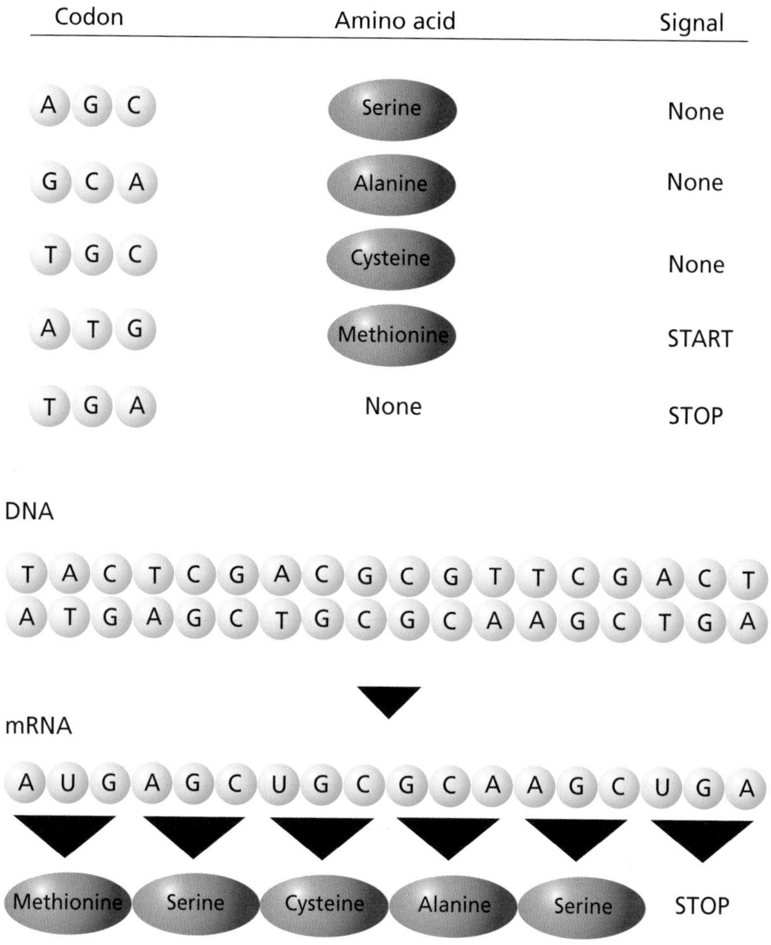

Codon	Amino acid	Signal
A G C	Serine	None
G C A	Alanine	None
T G C	Cysteine	None
A T G	Methionine	START
T G A	None	STOP

DNA

T A C T C G A C G C G T T C G A C T
A T G A G C T G C G C A A G C T G A

mRNA

A U G A G C U G C G C A A G C U G A

Methionine Serine Cysteine Alanine Serine STOP

© Infobase Publishing

The genetic code. Five nucleotide codons (blue beads) are shown, four specifying amino acids (red beads) and two that serve as start and stop signals. The codons, including the start and stop signals, are linked together to form a gene on the bottom, or coding, DNA strand. The coding strand is copied into messenger RNA (mRNA) in a process known as transcription. The mRNA is used to synthesize a protein from the amino acids in a process called translation. The abbreviations for the nucleotides are as follows: adenine (A), thymine (T), cytosine (C), and guanine (G). Note that in mRNA uracil (U) replaces the thymine (T) found in DNA.

THE UNIVERSAL GENETIC CODE

CODON	AMINO ACID	ABBREVIATIONS
GCA GCC GCG GCU	Alanine	A, Ala
AGA AGG CGA CGC CGG CGU	Arginine	R, Arg
AAC AAU	Asparagine	N, Asn
GAC GAU	Aspartic acid	D, Asp
UGC UGU	Cysteine	C, Cys
GAA GAG	Glutamic acid	E, Glu
CAA CAG	Glutamine	Q, Gln
GGA GGC GGG GGU	Glycine	G, Gly
CAC CAU	Histidine	H, His
AUA AUC AUU	Isoleucine	I, Ile
UUA UUG CUA CUC CUG CUU	Leucine	L, Leu
AAA AAG	Lysine	K, Lys
AUG	Methionine	M, Met
UUC UUU	Phenylalanine	F, Phe
CCA CCC CCG CCU	Proline	P, Pro
AGC AGU UCA UCC UCG UCU	Serine	S, Ser
UGG	Tryptophan	W, Trp
ACA ACC ACG ACU	Threonine	T, Thr
UAC UAU	Tyrosine	Y, Tyr
GUA GUC GUG GUU	Valine	V, Val
UAA UGA UAG	–	–

Codons are written using the standard abbreviation for each nucleotide on the messenger RNA: adenine (A), uracil (U), cytosine (C), and guanine (G). All but two of the amino acids (methionine and tryptophan) have more than one codon. The last codons (UAA, UGA, UAG) do not code for an amino acid but serve as stop signals. The AUG codon, in addition to specifying the amino acid methionine, also serves as a start codon. Note that in mRNA uracil replaces the thymine found in DNA.

around the world began sequencing individual genes from a variety of organisms, and the information obtained was used to study cell biology with unprecedented detail. It soon became obvious, however, that great advances in our understanding of human diseases, development, and physiology would come much quicker if human and animal genomes were sequenced as part of a large coordinated project.

THE HUMAN GENOME PROJECT

Sequencing the entire human genome is an idea that grew over a period of 20 years, beginning in the early 1980s. At that time, the Sanger sequencing method was but a few years old and had only been used to sequence viral or mitochondrial genomes. (Sequencing methods are discussed in chapter 10.) Indeed, one of the first genomes to be sequenced was that of bacteriophage G4, a virus that infects the bacterium *Escherichia coli (E. coli)*. The G4 genome consists of 5,577 nucleotide pairs (or base pairs, abbreviated bp) and was sequenced in Sanger's laboratory in 1979. By 1982, the Sanger protocol was used by others to sequence the genome of the animal virus SV40 (5,224 bp), the human mitochondrion (16,569 bp), and bacteriophage lambda (48,502 bp). Besides providing invaluable data, these projects demonstrated the feasibility of sequencing large genomes.

The possibility of sequencing the entire human genome was first discussed at scientific meetings organized by the U.S. Department of Energy (DOE) between 1984 and 1986. A committee appointed by the U.S. National Research Council (NRC) endorsed the idea in 1988 but recommended a broader program to include the sequencing of the genes of humans, bacteria, yeast, worms, flies, and mice. They also called for the establishment of research programs devoted to the ethical, legal, and social issues raised by human genome research. The program was formally launched in late 1990 as a consortium consisting of coordinated sequencing projects in the United States, Britain, France, Germany, Japan, and China. At

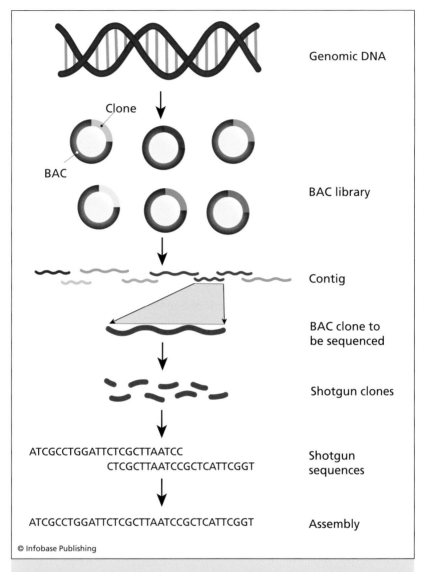

Genomic DNA

Clone

BAC

BAC library

Contig

BAC clone to be sequenced

Shotgun clones

ATCGCCTGGATTCTCGCTTAATCC
          CTCGCTTAATCCGCTCATTCGGT

Shotgun sequences

ATCGCCTGGATTCTCGCTTAATCCGCTCATTCGGT   Assembly

© Infobase Publishing

Shotgun sequencing. Total genomic DNA is cut with a restriction enzyme into one megabase (Mb) fragment (i.e., 1 million base pairs [bp] per fragment) that is cloned into bacterial artificial chromosomes (BACs) to form a library. The BAC fragments are partially character-ized in order to organize them into an overlapping assembly called a contig. Clones are selected from the contigs for shotgun sequencing and final assembly.

about the same time, the Human Genome Organization (HUGO) was founded to provide a forum for international coordination of genomic research.

By 1995, the consortium had established a strategy, called hierarchical shotgun sequencing, that they applied to the human genome as well as to the other organisms mentioned. With this strategy, genomic DNA is cut into one-megabase (Mb) fragments (i.e., each fragment consists of 1 million bases) that are cloned into bacterial artificial chromosomes (BACs) to form a library of DNA fragments. The BAC fragments are partially characterized, then organized into an overlapping assembly called a contig. Clones are selected from the contigs for shotgun sequencing. That is, each shotgun clone is digested into small 1,000 bp fragments, sequenced, and then assembled into the final sequence with the aid of computers. Organizing the initial BAC fragments into contigs greatly simplifies the final assembly stage.

Sequencing of the human genome was divided into two stages. The first stage, completed in 2001, was a rough draft that covered about 80 percent of the genome with an estimated size of more than 3 billion bases (also expressed as 3 gigabases, or 3 Gb). The final draft, completed in April 2003, covers the entire genome and refines the data for areas of the genome that were difficult to sequence. It also filled in many gaps that occurred in the rough draft. The human genome project was extended in 2009 with the formation of an international effort to sequence the genomes of thousands of individuals in order to gain a better understanding of genetic variations, particularly as they pertain to medical disorders, such as cancer or Alzheimer's disease. Human genomic information currently available may be divided into three categories: gene content, gene origins, and gene organization.

Gene Content

Analysis of the final draft has shown that the human genome consists of 3.2 Gb of DNA, encoding about 30,000 genes (estimates range between 25,000 to 32,000). Functions are known for only half of these genes. With an average size of 3,000 bases, the genes occupy only about 2 percent of the DNA, a result that was both unexpected and baffling. The human genome appears to be much larger than it needs to be. The vast regions of noncoding DNA, known as intervening sequences, have been the subject of much study and speculation. Some researchers believe that these regions do nothing at all and have taken to calling them "junk DNA." More creative minds have suggested that the intervening sequences are involved in the control of gene expression, the maintenance of chromosome structure, and the protection of genes from insertional mutagenesis (discussed below).

The estimated number of genes in the human genome is another surprising result. Some scientists, noting the complexity of the human brain and physiology, had predicted it would be closer to 100,000 genes. By comparison, the fruit fly has 13,338 genes and the simple roundworm, *Caenorhabditis elegans (C. elegans)*, has 18,266.

THE GENOMES OF SOME ANIMALS, PLANTS, AND MICROBES

ORGANISM	GENOME SIZE (BP)	NUMBER OF GENES
Human	3.2 billion	30,000
Laboratory mouse	2.6 billion	25,000
Mustard weed	100 million	25,000
Corn	2.5 billion	50,000
Roundworm	97 million	18,266
Fruit fly	137 million	13,338
Yeast	12.1 million	6,000
Bacterium	4.6 million	3,200
Human immuno-deficiency virus	9,700	9

These numbers seemed absurd, because they were so close to those of humans. But on reflection, the genome data suggests that human complexity, as compared to the fruit fly or the worm, is not simply due to the absolute number of genes but involves the complexity of the proteins that are encoded by those genes. In general, human proteins tend to be much more complex than those of lower organisms. Data from the final draft and other sources also provide a detailed overview of the functional profile of human cellular proteins.

Gene Origins

Fully one-half of human genes originated as transposable elements, also known as jumping genes (described below). Equally surprising is the fact that 220 of our genes were obtained by horizontal transfer from bacteria, rather than by ancestral, or vertical, inheritance. In other words, humans have obtained genes directly from bacteria, probably mediated by viral infections in a kind of natural gene therapy or gene swapping. Researchers know this to be the case because while these genes occur in bacteria, they are not present in yeast, fruit flies, or any other eukaryotes that have been tested.

The function of most of the horizontally transferred genes is unclear, although a few may code for basic metabolic enzymes. A notable exception is the *MAO* gene that codes for an enzyme called monoamine oxidase (MAO). (Gene and protein nomenclature is discussed in chapter 10.) Monoamines are neurotransmitters, such as dopamine, norepinephrine, and serotonin, which are needed for neural signaling in the human central nervous system. Monoamine oxidase plays a crucial role in the turnover of these neurotransmitters. How *MAO,* obtained from bacteria, could have developed such an important role in human physiology is a great mystery.

Gene Organization

In prokaryotes (bacteria), genes are simply arranged in tandem along a single chromosome, with little if any DNA separating one gene from the other. Each gene is transcribed into messenger RNA,

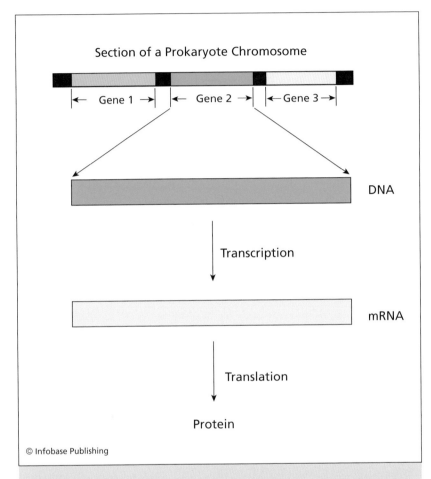

Prokaryote genes. The genes are arranged in tandem along the chromosome, with little, if any, DNA separating one gene from the other. The genes may code for protein, as shown above for gene 2, or ribosomal RNA (rRNA).

which is translated into protein. Indeed, in prokaryotes, which have no nucleus, translation often begins even before transcription is complete. In eukaryotes, as one might expect, gene organization is more complex. Data from the genome project shows clearly that eukaryote genes are split into subunits, called exons, and that each exon is separated by a length of DNA called an intron. A gene,

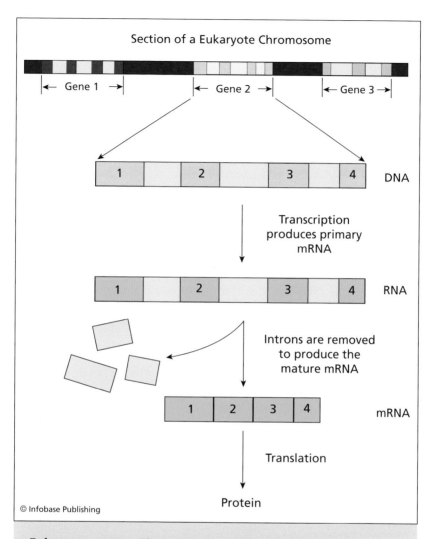

Section of a Eukaryote Chromosome

Gene 1   Gene 2   Gene 3

| 1 | | 2 | | 3 | | 4 | DNA

Transcription
produces primary
mRNA

| 1 | | 2 | | 3 | | 4 | RNA

Introns are removed
to produce the
mature mRNA

| 1 | 2 | 3 | 4 | mRNA

Translation

Protein

© Infobase Publishing

Eukaryote genes. The genes are arranged in separate subunits called exons (red, pale blue, or green) and introns (yellow). Each gene, which consists of introns and exons, is separated from other genes by long stretches of noncoding DNA called intervening sequences (dark blue). The genes are transcribed into a primary RNA molecule that includes exon and intron sequences. Nuclear enzymes remove the introns from the primary transcript, and the exons are then joined together to form the mature mRNA, which is translated into protein. Transcription of ribosomal genes is similar, except that the exons become the individual rRNAs.

consisting of introns and exons, is separated from other genes by the intervening sequences. Eukaryote genes are transcribed into a primary RNA molecule that includes exon and intron sequences. The primary transcript never leaves the nucleus and is never translated into protein. Nuclear enzymes remove the introns from the primary transcript, after which the exons are joined together to form the mature mRNA. Thus, only the exons carry the necessary code to produce a protein.

MOBILE GENETIC ELEMENTS

Mobile genetic elements are pieces of DNA, often containing whole genes, that are able to move from one chromosomal location to another. When first proposed by the American geneticist Barbara McClintock in 1951, the idea that genes could move from one location in the genome to some other location was greeted with disbelief and disdain. For more than 20 years, this brilliant idea languished in scientific limbo until the advent of recombinant technology made it possible to prove the existence of these wandering genes, also known as transposable genetic elements, transposons, and jumping genes. By the 1980s, McClintock's work was finally given the recognition it deserved, and in 1983, at the age of 81, she was awarded the Nobel Prize in physiology or medicine. She died on September 2, 1992.

McClintock's work provided several insights into the organization and evolution of the eukaryote genome: First, the position of some genes, within the genome, is flexible; second, the roles of transposable elements, introns, and intervening sequences are interconnected; and third, viruses are direct descendants of jumping genes. With the completion of the genome project, scientists now know that many of our genes were once transposable elements, including the 220 genes obtained by horizontal transfer from bacteria.

Jumping genes and viruses have been a driving force in the evolution of the human genome. As mentioned previously, genes account for only 2 percent of the genome; the rest is composed of noncoding DNA. Indeed, the genes themselves contain some noncoding DNA

Dr. Barbara McClintock (1902–92) in her cornfield at Cold Spring Harbor Laboratories in the 1950s. She received the Nobel Prize in physiology or medicine in 1983 for her discovery of transposable elements. *(Cold Spring Harbor Library and Archives)*

in the form of introns. Thus, it would seem that the human genome has evolved into a form that accommodates mobile genes. In such a genome, the odds of a transposable element damaging an existing gene when it inserts itself into a host's chromosome are extremely small. This type of genetic damage is known as insertional mutagenesis. When a jumping gene moves, it will, in all likelihood, reinsert into an intervening sequence where it may stay for thousands or millions of years. After having been duplicated, most transposons move again, producing many copies of the same gene sprinkled around the genome. These copies of the original gene are then free to mutate into other genes that may eventually become useful to the organism. Thus, copies of the original transposon are the source of many of the genes now present in the human genome.

The flexibility of a transposable genome is perhaps the single most important characteristic that led to the explosive adaptability of eukaryotes and the multicellular creatures they produced. Such a genome is essential for gene therapy, which attempts to cure a disease by introducing a normal gene into a patient's genome. If the human genome were organized like that of the prokaryotes, such a therapy would be nearly impossible.

Transposable elements have given us a flexible and extremely powerful genomic organization, but they have also given us viruses and all the illnesses they produce, such as AIDS, polio, and the common cold. Somehow, millions of years ago, a jumping gene learned how to jump right out of the cell. It acquired this ability in small steps as it moved from one place in the genome to another. A jumping gene that moves will usually reinsert into an intervening sequence. Occasionally, however, a transposon reinserts next to a gene, possibly one that codes for a protein that could serve as a capsid (i.e., a protein that protects a virus's genome and forms the overall structure of the viral particle). The next time such a transposon moved it could take a copy of the potential capsid gene with it. Eventually, by moving from place to place, the transposon collected a number of genes that made it possible for it to escape from the cell and to reinfect other cells. When that happened, a simple mobile genetic element went from being a molecular curiosity to a living thing, equipped with a life cycle and the power of reproduction.

GENE MUTATIONS

DNA is a very stable macromolecule, but it is not immutable. Scientists have estimated that for any genome, one nucleotide in a billion will be altered or damaged each time the DNA is replicated. In the human genome, this amounts to three mutations each time a cell divides. These mutations can be beneficial, neutral, or lethal. Beneficial mutations drove the transformation of the first cells, which appeared on Earth 3.5 billion years ago, into the wide variety of multicellular life that exists today. These mutations made it possible for the prokaryotes to evolve into the eukaryotes and for the eukaryotes to produce the cell-signaling hardware necessary for the production of plants and animals.

Gene mutations are thus an essential aspect of evolutionary change, but they can also be a major headache for individual organisms. Many mutations produce debilitating diseases or are outright lethal, killing the individual during embryogenesis or soon after birth. As mentioned above, the natural mutation rate is very low, but environmental pollutants, insertional mutagenesis, and certain kinds of radiation can increase the rate up to a thousandfold. Mutations can alter the DNA in four different ways: by altering a single nucleotide (a point mutation), inverting a segment of DNA (an inversion), deleting a segment of DNA (a deletion), or by translocating a segment of DNA from one chromosome to another chromosome (a translocation).

A point mutation affects a single nucleotide, giving rise to a new codon. For example, TGC is the codon for the amino acid cysteine. If a mutation alters the G nucleotide to a T, the new codon, TTC, specifies phenylalanine instead of cysteine. Thus, in the example shown in the figure on page 9, the protein sequence would change from methionine-serine-cysteine-alanine-serine to methionine-serine-phenylalanine-alanine-serine. This difference of a single amino acid is often enough to destroy the normal function of a protein, even if it consists of 500 amino acids.

In some cases, a point mutation can destroy a crucial localization sequence that is present on many proteins. Some proteins are destined for the nucleus, some are supposed to stay in the cytoplasm, while others must travel a special route, involving the endoplasmic reticulum and the Golgi apparatus, which takes them to the cell membrane. The localization sequence is used by the cell's machinery to ensure that each protein is sent to its proper destination. The default destination (i.e., no localization sequence) is the cytoplasm. A well-studied example is the nuclear localization sequence (NLS), located at one end of the protein, which serves as a passport to the nucleus. A common NLS is lysine-lysine-lysine-arginine-lysine. A nuclear protein with a mutated NLS, such as lysine-threonine-lysine-arginine-lysine, is blocked from entering the nucleus.

Scientists have provided direct evidence for this remarkable process by adding an NLS to proteins that are not supposed to be in the nucleus. In every case, cytoplasmic proteins tagged with an NLS end up in the nucleus. Proteins destined for the cell membrane carry a membrane localization sequence. If this sequence is missing or mutated, the protein is left in the cytoplasm. Thus, in cases such as these, a mutated protein may retain a normal function but end up in the wrong compartment. Cystic fibrosis, discussed in the next chapter, is produced in this way.

Point mutations can have a dramatic effect on the normal behavior of many kinds of proteins. In one case, a mutation in a protein that serves as a receptor for epidermal growth factor (EGF) keeps the receptor in an activated state even in the absence of EGF. This has the effect of driving the cell to divide uncontrollably, leading to the formation of a cancerous growth. Mutations such as these are found in human brain tumors called glioblastomas. Point mutations are also known to cripple the behavior of many crucial cellular enzymes, such as adenosine deaminase (discussed in chapter 4) and ornithine transcarbamylase (discussed in chapter 5). These mutations produce debilitating diseases that were among the first to be treated with gene therapy.

Point mutations can also affect the expression of a gene without damaging the gene product. This occurs when the promoter is altered instead of the coding region. When this happens, the gene may be turned on permanently. An example of this type of mutation involves a proto-oncogene called *Myc* (pronounced "mick"). This gene codes for a protein that is involved in stimulating cell growth and proliferation. When its promoter is mutated, the Myc protein is produced at abnormally high rates, thus forcing the cell to reproduce inappropriately. This type of mutation is common in a cancer known as Burkitt's lymphoma.

Inversions, deletions, and translocations are all commonly encountered in cancer cells. These mutations lead to extensive genetic

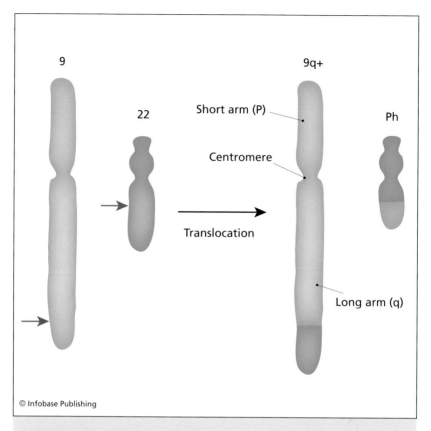

Philadelphia chromosome (Ph). This chromosome is produced by a translocation between the long arms of chromosomes 9 and 22. Red arrows mark the fragmentation points. The notation "9q+" indicates an addition to the long arm of chromosome 9. The chromosomes are aligned at the centromeres.

damage, sometimes corrupting the entire genome. The most famous mutation of this kind is the Philadelphia chromosome, named after the city where it was first discovered. This chromosomal abnormality, involving a translocation between the long arms of chromosomes 9 and 22, is associated with chronic myelogenous leukemia and can be found in the leukemic white blood cells of virtually every patient suffering from this form of cancer.

SUMMARY

For biologists, the human genome is the final frontier. The DNA that inhabits the nucleus of every cell in the body orchestrates our evolution, our behavior, our longevity, and our resistance to disease. The availability of rapid DNA sequences has given us the complete sequence of the human genome and the genomes of many other organisms. Analysis of this data has provided the exact sequence and location of most of our genes and a much greater understanding of how the genome is organized. Mobile genetic elements, viruses, and bacteria have played major roles in shaping the organization and composition of the human genome. Gene mutations can now be studied in detail, both for the purpose of explaining the clinical symptoms of a genetic disease and for designing a therapy. These mutations and the therapies that have been developed to treat them are the main focus of this book.

2

Genetic Disorders

When a gene is damaged, it usually is caused by a point mutation, a change that affects a single nucleotide. Sickle-cell anemia, a disease affecting red blood cells, was the first genetic disorder of this kind to be described. The mutation occurs in a gene that codes for the beta chain of hemoglobin, converting the codon GAG to GTG, and resulting in a protein that has the amino acid valine at position 6, instead of glutamic acid. It may seem like an insignificant difference, but this single amino-acid substitution is enough to cripple the hemoglobin molecule, making it impossible for it to carry enough oxygen to meet the demands of a normal adult.

Sickle-cell anemia, like many genetic disorders, is monogenic, being caused by a single defective gene. But many forms of cancer and some neurological disorders are polygenic, involving several mutated

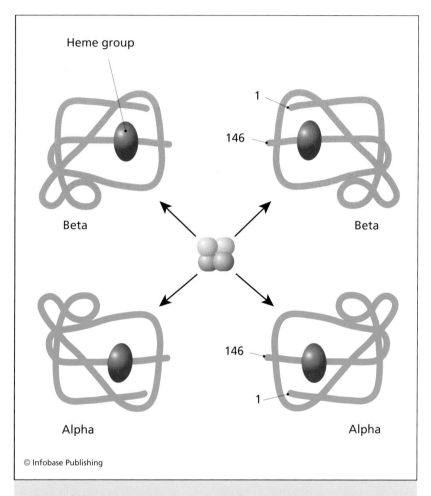

Hemoglobin. The molecule consists of two alpha and two beta protein chains, each bound to an iron-containing heme group that carries oxygen. The positions of the first and last amino acids (1 and 146) are indicated. Ancestral hemoglobin probably consisted of a single alpha or beta chain.

genes. The genetic disorders described in this chapter are of both kinds and are being treated in clinical trials or will be in the near future. Taken together, these diseases account for more than 200,000 deaths in North America each year. Although the range of ailments treatable with gene therapy is extremely broad, more than 65 percent of the clinical trials are aimed at curing various forms of cancer.

CANCER

Most of the gene therapy trials in progress today are aimed at curing or at least controlling various forms of cancer. In general, the trials tend to focus on the most common types of cancer, such as those affecting the breast, colon, prostate gland, and skin.

Breast Cancer

Breast cancer, like all cancers, is a genetic disorder caused by a mutation in one or more genes. Viruses cause some cancers, but the mechanism still involves a corruption of genetic information equivalent to a naturally occurring mutation.

Breast cancer is the second major cause of cancer death in women around the world, with an estimated 50,000 deaths per year in the United States alone. Two genes, *Brca1* (breast cancer 1), located on chromosome 17, and *Brca2*, on chromosome 13, were isolated in 1994. Mutations in either of these genes are associated with the occurrence of breast and ovarian cancer. The proteins produced by these genes are involved in repairing damage to DNA, and their loss can lead to a buildup of errors in DNA replication, which can lead to cancerous growths. Extensive analysis of the human genome has identified other genes that may be involved in this type of cancer. Researchers in Cambridge, England, and at the Harvard School of Public Health in the United States have identified six new genetic sites that increase the risk of breast cancer. Additional research will be required to determine the function of these new genes and genetic elements. An American research team, led by Bert Vogelstein and Kenneth Kinzler, concluded from a recent genomewide study that at least 200 genes are involved in the development of breast cancer.

General screening of the population for *Brca1*, *Brca2*, and the newly identified genes is not yet recommended, but several clinical

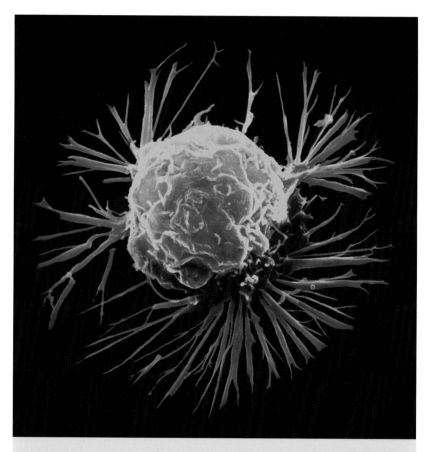

Colored scanning electron micrograph (SEM) of a single breast cancer cell. The SEM shows the cell's uneven surface and cytoplasmic projections. Clumps of cancerous (malignant) cells form tumors, which possess the ability to invade and destroy surrounding tissues and travel to distant parts of the body to seed secondary tumors. Breast cancer is the most common cause of cancer in women. Magnification: unknown. *(NCI/Photo Researchers, Inc.)*

gene therapy trials are under way that are attempting to replace or supplement mutated genes with normal copies. Some of the trials are also attempting to introduce tumor-suppressor genes into breast cells to block development of the cancerous growths.

Colon Cancer

Colon cancer strikes more than 100,000 people every year in North America with about 50,000 resulting deaths. Actively dividing cells, such as those that line the colon, are especially prone to cancer development because of errors that can occur when DNA is replicated. Environmental factors, such as diet and cigarette smoke, play a role, but two genes have been identified that can make an individual especially susceptible. One of these genes, called *Msh2,* is located on chromosome 2, and the second, *Mlh1,* is on chromosome 3. Patients carrying mutations in either of these genes are typically diagnosed with colon cancer before the age of 50. *Mlh1* and *Msh2* code for proteins that are involved in post-replicative mismatch repair of DNA. The loss of these repair enzymes leads to a genomewide accumulation of multiple point mutations, favoring cancer development. Researchers at Johns Hopkins Kimmel Cancer Center, led by Kenneth Kinzler and Bert Vogelstein, have recently identified nearly 200 genes that are associated with the onset of colon cancer. The function of these new genes is unknown, but as with breast cancer the sheer number of genes greatly complicates the development of an effective therapy.

Prostate Cancer

The prostate gland is part of the male reproductive system. It makes and stores portions of the seminal fluid, a fluid that is mixed with sperm to produce semen. The gland is about the size of a walnut and is located below the bladder near the base of the penis. It surrounds the upper part of the urethra, the tube that empties urine from the bladder. Because of its location, abnormal growth of the prostate can pinch the urethra, blocking the flow of urine. The prostate gland is regulated by the male sex hormone, testosterone.

Prostate cancer is the most common type of cancer in North American men other than skin cancer. The number of men affected by prostate cancer is nearly equal to the number of women affected by breast cancer, but the mortality of prostate cancer is lower. Age, family history, and diet are the main risk factors. Prostate cancer usually occurs in men over the age of 55. The average age of patients at the time of diagnosis is 70. A man's risk of developing prostate cancer is higher if his father or brother has had the disease. This disease is much more common in African Americans than in whites and is less common in Asians and American Indians. Some evidence suggests that a diet high in animal fat may increase the risk of prostate cancer and a diet high in fruits and vegetables may decrease the risk. Common symptoms of prostate cancer are a need to urinate frequently, especially at night; difficulty starting urination or holding back urine; inability to urinate; weak or interrupted flow of urine; painful or burning urination; difficulty in having an erection; painful ejaculation; blood in urine or semen; or, in advanced stages, frequent pain or stiffness in the lower back, hips, or upper thighs.

Researchers in Iceland, led by Kari Stefansson, after conducting a genomewide screen of more than 23,000 Icelanders, have identified two DNA regions, located on chromosome 5 and chromosome 8, that are strongly associated with the development of prostate cancer.

Skin Cancer

The skin protects us against heat, light, injury, and infection. It helps regulate body temperature and stores water, fat, and vitamin D. This tissue is made up of two main layers: the outer epidermis and the inner dermis. The epidermis (outer layer of the skin) is mostly made up of flat, scalelike cells called squamous cells. Under the squamous cells are round cells called basal cells. The deepest part of the epidermis also contains melanocytes, cells that produce melanin, which gives the skin its color. The dermis (just below the epidermis) contains blood and lymph vessels, hair follicles, and glands. These glands produce sweat to regulate body temperature and sebum, an oily substance that helps keep the skin from drying out. Sweat and sebum reach the skin's surface through tiny openings called pores.

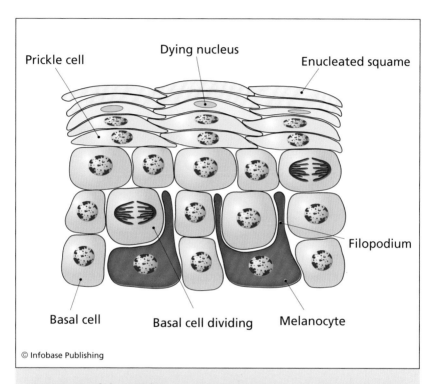

© Infobase Publishing

Structure of the epidermis. The epidermis is a stratified epithelium that forms the outer layer of the skin—it consists of three cell populations: squamous cells (the enucleated squames and the prickle cells), the cuboidal basal cells, and, at the deepest layers, pigment-containing melanocytes. The basal and squamous cell layers are in a constant state of change. Division of a basal cell is followed by keratinization, a process by which the daughter cells are transformed into prickle cells. Keratin is a tough protein that makes the outer cell layer resistant to abrasion. In the final stage of keratinization, the prickle cell loses its nucleus. The now dead and fully keratinized squame eventually flakes off from the surface. Keratinized squames from the scalp are called dandruff.

This is the most common type of cancer in North America, with 1 million cases diagnosed each year. Nearly half of the North American population will develop some form of skin cancer by the time they reach 65. The two most common kinds of skin cancer are basal cell carcinoma and squamous cell carcinoma. Basal cell carcinoma accounts for more than 90 percent of all skin cancers in North America. It is a slow-growing cancer that seldom spreads to other parts of the body. Squamous cell carcinoma also rarely spreads, but it does so more often than basal cell carcinoma. Another type of cancer that occurs in the skin is melanoma, which begins in the melanocytes. Melanomas are quick to metastasize and are often deadly. Every year, more than 62,000 people in North America are diagnosed with melanoma, the most aggressive form of skin cancer, and of those diagnosed more than 8,400 will die from this disease. Melanoma is often initiated by overexposure to sunlight, and although remission under treatment is common, the risk of recurrence is very high. Basal cell carcinoma and squamous cell carcinoma are sometimes called nonmelanoma skin cancer.

Although anyone can get skin cancer, the risk is greatest for people who have fair skin that freckles easily, often those with red or blond hair and blue or light-colored eyes. The primary risk factor is excessive exposure to ultraviolet (UV) radiation. The use of sunscreens (particularly on children), hats, and protective clothing are strongly recommended for lengthy outdoor excursions. The most common warning sign of skin cancer is a growth or a sore that does not heal. Skin cancers vary considerably in the way they look. Some begin as a pale waxy lump, whereas others first appear as a firm red lump. Sometimes, the lump bleeds or develops a crust. Skin cancer can also start as a flat, red spot that is rough, dry, or scaly. Both basal and squamous cell cancers are found on areas of the skin that are exposed to the sun: the face, neck, hands, and arms. Actinic keratosis, which appears as rough, red or brown scaly patches on the

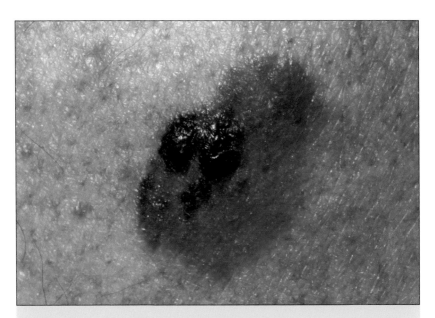

Malignant melanoma. Close-up of the skin of a 71-year-old man that shows the growth of a malignant melanoma (dark area). Melanomas are tumors of the pigment-producing cells of the skin, or melanocytes. They may contain melanin (as here) or be free of pigment. They usually grow from an existing mole (or nevus), often after prolonged exposure to the ultraviolet radiation in sunlight. The mole may enlarge, become lumpy, change color, spread, bleed, or itch. Early diagnosis and treatment are essential to prevent the spread of the cancer to the lymph nodes and liver, which is generally fatal. If they are caught early, they can be excised or treated with drugs. *(Dr. P. Marazzi/Photo Researchers, Inc.)*

skin, is known as a precancerous condition because it sometimes develops into squamous cell cancer.

A mutation in a gene on chromosome 9, known as *Cyclin dependent kinase N2 (Cdkn2),* makes the carrier more susceptible to this form of cancer. *Cdkn2* codes for a protein called P16 that is an important regulator of the cell division cycle, in particular, the timing of DNA synthesis. A defective P16 allows uncontrolled cell division, which is a common characteristic of melanoma and cancer cells in general. Uncontrolled proliferation of the skin is usually apparent with the appearance of dark, irregular-shaped moles, appearing on the nose, forehead, and upper torso.

Prevention is the first strategy against this cancer, by using protective clothing and sunscreen. Conventional treatments involve surgical removal of the tumors and radiation therapy. Several gene therapy trials are under way with the aim of replacing or supplementing the mutated *P16* gene with a normal copy. In addition, some trials are attempting to introduce nonspecific antitumor genes that will stimulate the immune system to destroy tumor cells.

Scientists at the National Cancer Institute in the United States have identified a new genetic risk factor for melanoma. People with fair skin are generally at increased risk of developing melanoma. Differences in skin color, or pigmentation, are due largely to the *Melanocortin-1 receptor (Mc1r)* gene. Everyone has two copies of *Mc1r;* one inherited from the mother and one from the father, and either can be the standard form or a variant. Some variant forms of *Mc1r* are responsible for traits such as fair skin, freckling, and red hair. Genetic variations in this gene may reduce the effectiveness of the UV-blocking function of melanin leading to extensive UV-induced genetic damage and with it the elevated risk of developing skin cancer.

CARDIOVASCULAR DISEASE

Atherosclerosis is a disease of the arteries that can strike at any age, although it is not a serious threat until people who are susceptible to it reach their 40s or 50s. This disease is characterized by a narrowing of the arteries, caused by the formation of plaques containing cells and cholesterol. Several factors influence the appearance of plaques, including high levels of cholesterol (and cholesterol precursors, such as triglyceride) in the blood, high blood pressure, and cigarette smoke.

Apolipoprotein E, encoded by a gene on chromosome 19, removes excess cholesterol from the blood by delivering it to liver cells, which store it for later use. Mutant apolipoprotein loses the ability to bind to liver receptors, resulting in a buildup of cholesterol in the blood. Several mutated forms of apolipoprotein E are known to occur, and these need to be studied in detail before this disease can be treated with gene therapy.

A second form of cardiovascular disease, affecting the coronary arteries, is currently being treated with gene therapy. Coronary arteries carry blood to the myocytes, or heart muscle cells, and if they become blocked or otherwise damaged the cells die from lack of oxygen. In serious cases, this can lead to a massive heart attack and death of the patient. In milder cases, damage to the heart is minimal, but coronary circulation is insufficient to allow the patient a normal lifestyle. Gene therapy is attempting to help this group of patients by introducing directly into the heart a gene that codes for vascular endothelial growth factor (VEGF), a growth factor that stimulates both the growth and repair of the coronary arteries, in order to reestablish an adequate blood flow. Although this form of therapy shows great promise, it is currently at an early stage of development.

CYSTIC FIBROSIS

Of all the genetic diseases, cystic fibrosis (CF) is the most debilitating. This disease is associated with the production of thick, sticky mucus that clogs the lungs, making breathing difficult and providing an environment that is susceptible to bacterial infection. Indeed, most sufferers of CF die of congestive lung failure, brought on by a bacterial infection, before the age of 30.

CF is caused by a mutation in a gene that codes for a sodium chloride transporter, called CFTR, found on the surface of the epithelial cells that line the lungs and other organs. The first mutation was discovered in 1989, and since then many other mutations have been identified, all of which result in defective transport of sodium and chloride by bronchial and lung epithelial cells. The transporter can tolerate some amino acid substitutions, so the severity of the disease varies depending on the site of the mutation. The most common mutation, involving the loss of phenylalanine at position 508, does not cripple the transporter, but it does alter its three-dimensional shape, and, as a consequence, the sorting machinery in the Golgi complex never delivers it to the cell membrane. (The eukaryote cell and the function of the Golgi complex are described in chapter 10.)

The loss of the CF transporter reduces the amount of water on the cell surface, thus increasing both the density of the mucus layer and the acidity inside the cell. The abnormal acid level leads to the production of a defective glycocalyx that is unable to repel bacteria; as a consequence, a specific bacterium, *Pseudomonas aeruginosa,* is free to infect and destroy lung tissue. Conventional treatments are available that thin the mucus layer and kill *Pseudomonas,* but they are only partially successful. Patients suffering from CF must undergo regular treatment to dislodge the mucus in order to clear the airways, and for them life is a daily battle against suffocation.

The *CFTR* gene was mapped to the long arm of chromosome 7 in 1985 and cloned in 1990. Many gene therapy trials are under way, and, because CF is a monogenic disorder, hopes are high that a cure will be possible in the near future.

HEMOPHILIA

A remarkable thing happens whenever one cuts oneself: Some of the blood, which is normally a liquid, is converted to a fibrous solid at the site of the wound. The blood clot, so formed, has several functions: It reduces blood loss, it covers the wound to prevent bacterial infection, and it provides a temporary patch until the cells repair the damage. The formation of a blood clot is a complex process that involves at least a dozen enzymes and protein factors. The principal elements in the clotting process are the proteins prothrombin,

thrombin, and fibrinogen. These proteins are modified in sequence, with the help of several clotting factors, to produce fibrin, the protein from which clots are made.

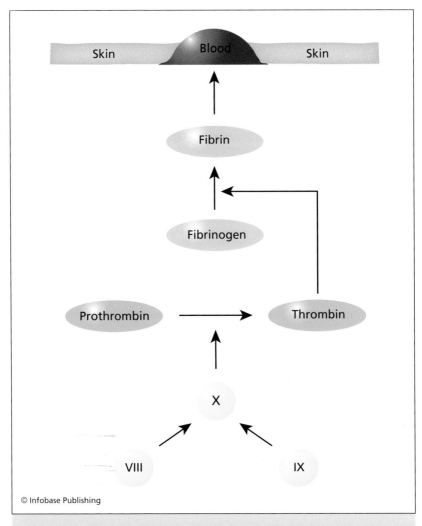

Formation of a blood clot. Two clotting factors (VIII and IX) activate a third (X), which stimulates conversion of prothrombin to thrombin. Thrombin then catalyzes the conversion of fibrinogen to fibrin to convert the drop of blood, collecting at a wound, to a solid clot.

Hemophilia A is a disease characterized by a failure of the clotting process. It is caused by a mutation in the clotting factor VIII gene (known as *F8*), located on the long arm of the X chromosome, which affects one in 5,000 males. A second and much rarer form of this disease (hemophilia B) is due to the loss of clotting factor IX. Hemophilia B is sometimes called Christmas disease after Stephen Christmas, the first patient to be diagnosed with this form of hemophilia, and for a time factor IX was called the Christmas factor. The factor IX gene *(F9)* is located on the long arm of the X chromosome close to *F8*. Both clotting factors, VIII and IX, are synthesized in the liver.

A famous carrier of hemophilia A was Queen Victoria, who transmitted it through the birth and marriage of her many children to the royal families of Germany, Spain, and Russia. Males are susceptible to this disease because they have only one X chromosome. Females, with two X chromosomes, are not likely to have a defective *F8* gene on both chromosomes and so rarely show the symptoms of this disease.

Conventional treatment of hemophilia A has involved regular transfusions of normal blood to replace the defective clotting factor, but this was a major inconvenience and often led to liver damage. Contamination of human blood supplies with the AIDS virus and the resulting infection of many hemophiliacs in the 1980s forced the development of alternate sources of factor VIII for replacement therapy, including antibody-purified factors and the production of factor VIII using DNA recombinant technology. These procedures produce safe, high-quality clotting factors but are extremely expensive.

Gene therapy trials, involving factor VIII gene transfer to liver and bone marrow cells in experimental animals, have not resulted in sustained production of the clotting factor. A recent attempt to introduce the gene into gut epithelia appears to be more successful and may soon lead to human clinical trials. Gene therapy trials involving factor IX have been more successful, and a cure for this form of hemophilia may be found in the near future.

IMMUNE DEFICIENCIES

All animals have an immune system that is designed to combat invading microbes without which many diseases cause death. Our immune system consists of a large population of white blood cells that appear in many different forms, the most important of which are the B cells, T cells, and macrophages. B and T cells are lymphocytes that develop in bone marrow and the thymus, respectively. Macrophages are phagocytic blood cells—they confront invaders head-on by eating them. B cells attack foreign material indirectly by producing antibodies, and T cells control and coordinate the immune response by releasing signaling molecules called cytokines that recruit macrophages and B cells. T cells also have the remarkable ability to detect invaders that are hiding inside a cell. Even more remarkable, they can force the infected cell to commit suicide in order to control the spread of the infection.

A common form of immune deficiency is severe combined immunodeficiency-X1 (SCID-X1). This disease represents a group of rare, sometimes fatal, disorders that destroy the immune response. Without special precautions, the patients die during their first year of life. Those who survive are susceptible to repeated bouts of pneumonia, meningitis, and chicken pox.

All forms of SCID are inherited, with as many as half of the cases being linked to the X chromosome. The mother passes on this disease, since males born with this disorder usually die before reaching their reproductive years. SCID-X1 results from a mutation that cripples a receptor for a cytokine called interleukin 2 (the *IL2R* gene). The IL2R protein activates an important signaling molecule called Janus kinase 3 (JAK3). A mutation in the *JAK3* gene, located on chromosome 19, can result in a second form of SCID. Defective cytokine receptors and the signaling pathways they activate prevent the normal development of T lymphocytes that play a key role in identifying invading agents as well as activating other members of the immune system.

A third form of SCID is due to a mutation in the *Adenosine deaminase (ADA)* gene located on chromosome 20. This gene is active in T lymphocytes, and the mutation leads to a toxic buildup of adenosine inside the cell, thus blocking the normal maturation and activity of this crucial member of the immune system. Some patients suffering from ADA deficiency can mount a weak immune response, but in most cases the response is abolished. The conventional treatment, involving a bone marrow transplant, has been successful in saving many lives, but acquiring a compatible tissue match for every patient is extremely difficult and sometimes impossible.

In many ways, SCID is an ideal candidate for gene therapy since the T cells can be collected from the patient and grown in culture, where the healthy gene is inserted and tested. If the T cells take up the gene and express it properly, they can then be injected into the bloodstream of the patient. It is for this reason that the very first gene therapy trial (discussed in chapter 4) involved a young patient suffering from ADA deficiency. That trial was a success, and a more recent trial, involving SCID-X1, has also reported success in curing this form of immune deficiency.

LIVER DISEASE

Proteins that one eats for food are broken down (catabolized) to amino acids, which may be used to generate energy or to construct other proteins. A major by-product in the catabolism of amino acids is ammonia, the stuff of Earth's ancient atmosphere and a molecule that in high concentrations is toxic. Cells deal with the toxicity by converting the ammonia to urea, a much safer molecule that passes out of our bodies as urine. The production of urea depends on the liver enzyme ornithine transcarbamylase (OTC). If OTC is defective, blood levels of ammonia increase rapidly, resulting in coma, brain damage, and death.

The gene for OTC has been isolated and localized to the X chromosome. Accordingly, this disease, like hemophilia, affects mostly males. Some males show a partial deficiency in OTC due to somatic cell mosaicism; that is, some of the liver cells produce the normal enzyme. Traditional treatment involves a rigid diet and constant monitoring of blood ammonia levels. But this approach has only been partially effective and often leads to repeated comas, each of which carries a 15 percent risk of mortality or brain damage. Because OTC is expressed exclusively in the liver, where general detoxification of the blood occurs, liver transplants have been attempted, but with little success.

Being monogenic, with a single organ affected, this disease is an ideal candidate for gene therapy. However, a clinical trial in 1999 designed to cure this disease ended in disaster, bringing all other trials to a halt for more than a year. (See chapter 5 for a detailed discussion of this trial.) Further trials are now underway with a new set of guidelines and protocols, and expectations are high that gene therapy will be able to cure this disease in the near future.

MUSCULAR DYSTROPHY

Muscular dystrophy, also called Duchene muscular dystrophy (DMD), is one of a group of disorders characterized by a pathological swelling of skeletal muscles. It is caused by a mutation in the *Dmd* gene, located on the X chromosome. DMD is the most prevalent form of this disease, occurring early in life and affecting nearly a million boys worldwide.

The gene for DMD codes for a protein called dystrophin, which is thought to strengthen muscle cells by anchoring the cytoskeleton to the surface membrane. Without dystrophin, the cell membrane becomes permeable to fluid entry, causing the cell to swell until it ruptures from the high internal pressure.

Researchers have developed a mouse model for DMD in an attempt to better understand the role of dystrophin in muscle physiology. Gene therapy trials will attempt to replace the mutated dystrophin or introduce the closely related utrophin in order to stabilize the cell's membranes.

NEUROLOGICAL DISORDERS

The human central nervous system (CNS) consists of the brain and the spinal cord. The main part of the brain is called the cerebrum, which is the home of human intellect and the source of individual personality; it also processes and analyzes information from all the sensory nerves of the body. The cerebrum consists of two morphologically identical cerebral hemispheres, connected by a thick bundle of nerves called the corpus callosum. All of the nerve cell bodies are located in the outer layer of the cerebrum called the cerebral cortex. A special area of the cerebrum called the hippocampus is important for processing memories for long-term storage in other parts of the brain. The cerebellum regulates fine motor control over our muscles, making it possible for a person to learn how to play the piano, knit a sweater, and perform other activities that require intricate coordination. The brain stem is in control of our automatic functions, such as the rate at which the heart beats, the contraction of muscles of the digestive tract, and the respiratory rate. It also controls our ability to sleep and to stay awake.

Alzheimer's Disease

Alzheimer's disease (AD) is a devastating neurological disorder that leads to a progressive loss of memory, language, and the ability to recognize friends and family. AD begins in the basal cerebral cortex, quickly spreading to the hippocampus. During the early stages, known as preclinical AD, some damage occurs to the brain but not enough to produce outward signs of the disease. Over a period of years, AD spreads to many areas of the cerebrum, but it does not affect the cerebellum or the brain stem.

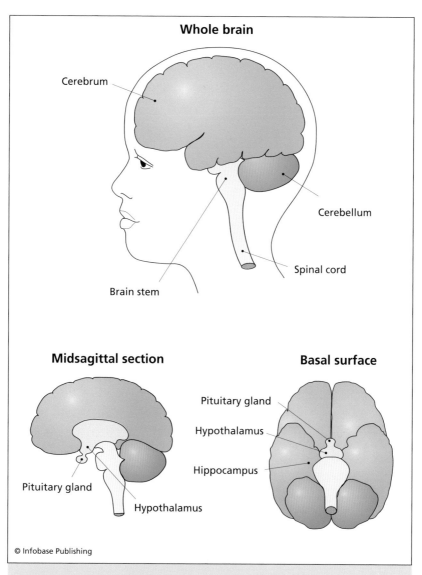

Whole brain

Cerebrum

Cerebellum

Spinal cord

Brain stem

Midsagittal section

Pituitary gland

Hypothalamus

Basal surface

Pituitary gland

Hypothalamus

Hippocampus

© Infobase Publishing

Human central nervous system. The human brain consists of the cerebrum, the cerebellum, and the brain stem, which is continuous with the spinal cord. The brain and spinal cord are called the central nervous system (CNS). The pituitary gland, a crucial part of the neuroendocrine system, is connected to the hypothalamus at the base of the brain (midsagittal section). The hippocampus, located on the basal surface of the brain, coordinates memory functions.

The average time course of the disease, from early symptoms to complete loss of cognition, is 10 years. Alois Alzheimer first described AD in 1907, and this neurological disease has since become

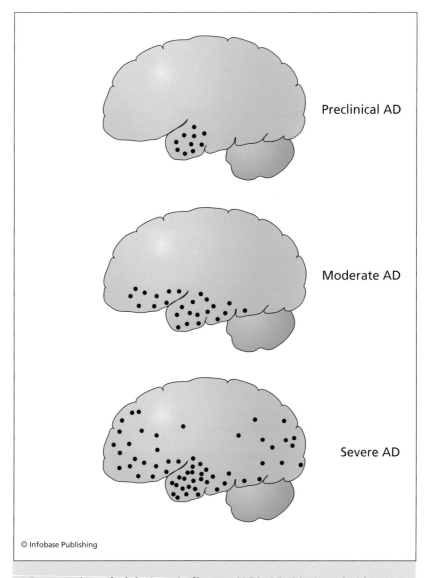

© Infobase Publishing

Progression of Alzheimer's disease (AD). AD (black circles) begins in the hippocampus, spreading over a period of years to affect several regions of the cerebrum.

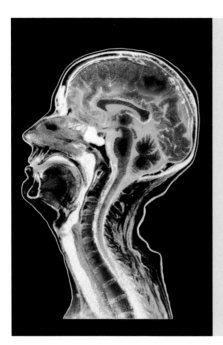

Colored magnetic resonance imaging (MRI) scan of a sagittal section through the brain of a 51-year-old male, showing cerebral atrophy. Atrophy of parts of the cerebrum of the brain occurs in various disorders, including stroke, AD, and AIDS dementia. Here the area of the upper cerebrum affected by atrophy is colored dark red. Atrophy is shrinkage and wasting away of tissue. In stroke, brain cells die due to deprived blood supply to the brain; in Alzheimer's disease, the brain shrinks leading to senile dementia. *(Simon Fraser/ Photo Researchers, Inc.)*

the fourth leading cause of death among the elderly. The incidence of AD increases with age and is twice as common in women than it is in men.

AD is a polygenic disease that tends to run in families and involves mutations in four genes that are located on chromosomes 1, 14, 19, and 21. The best characterized, being the subject of many studies, are *AD3* on chromosome 14 and *AD4* on chromosome 1. These genes code for related cell-surface signaling proteins called amyloids, which, when mutated, become neurotoxins. A major characteristic of this disease is the formation of lesions, or wounds, made of fragmented brain cells surrounded by amyloid proteins. These lesions and their associated proteins are closely related to structures found in patients suffering from Down's syndrome, all of whom are affected by this disease.

Many scientists believe that AD is a single disease with a common metabolic amyloid pathway. That is, the four genetic loci associated with this disease all lead, when mutated, to the production of similar neurotoxic amyloid proteins. Gene therapy trials for this disease are currently focused on introducing a gene coding for nerve growth factor.

Parkinson's Disease

This neurological disorder was first described by James Parkinson in 1817 and since then has become a serious health problem, with more than half a million North Americans affected at any one time. Most people are more than 50 years old when the disease appears, although it can occur in younger patients. This is a neurodegenerative disease that is associated with the development of a tremor, muscular stiffness, and loss of balance. These conditions often make it difficult for the patient to stand and walk. A typical feature of this disease is the presence of cellular debris, which consists of degenerating neurons, in several regions of the brain.

Until recently, Parkinson's disease was not thought to be heritable, and research was focused on environmental risk factors such as viral infection or neurotoxins. However, a candidate gene for some cases of Parkinson's disease was mapped to chromosome 4, and mutations in this gene have now been linked to several Parkinson's disease families. The product of this gene is a protein called alpha-synuclein, which may also be involved in the development of Alzheimer's disease.

Since alpha-synuclein is implicated in both Parkinson's and Alzheimer's diseases, there may be similar pathogenic mechanisms shared between the two. However, the function of this protein is not known, and for this reason gene therapy trials have adopted a general strategy involving nerve growth factors to try and rescue dying neurons.

Huntington's Disease

Huntington's disease (HD) is an inherited neurological disease that leads to dementia in more than 30,000 North Americans every year. In addition, it has been estimated that 150,000 people are at risk of inheriting HD from their parents.

The HD gene was mapped to chromosome 4 in 1983 and cloned in 1993. The mutation is an expansion of a nucleotide triplet repeat (CAG-CAG-) in the DNA that codes for the protein Huntingtin. People who have the expanded CAG repeats always suffer from Huntington's disease, but the function of the gene product is not known. With the discovery of the HD gene, a test was developed that allows those at risk to find out whether or not they will develop the disease. Animal models have also been developed, and investigators know that mice have a gene that is similar to the human HD gene. Gene therapy trials for HD are in the planning stage.

VISION IMPAIRMENT

A common vision disorder, known as Leber congenital amaurosis, is associated with the degeneration of the retina. This disease is caused by a point mutation in the *RPE65* gene, which codes for a protein (RPE65) that is essential for the normal functioning of the retina, located at the back of the eye.

The eye is like a camera that focuses an image onto a piece of film. It has an aperture (the pupil) that is regulated by the iris to vary the amount of light entering the eye, and it has a flexible lens that, with the aid of attached muscles, can alter its focal length so objects can be seen clearly whether they are inches or yards away. The interior of the eyeball is filled with a clear, viscous fluid called vitreous humor, which has the same refractive index as the lens. This minimizes the amount of scattered light to ensure the image is brought to a sharp focus on the retina. A small area near the center of the retina, called the fovea, is the place where the image is in the sharpest focus.

The retina is a thin layer of nervous tissue, about the thickness of a fingernail, that receives and processes images before sending them on to the visual cortex at the back of the brain. This tissue is composed of four kinds of neurons: photoreceptors, interneurons, ganglion cells, and horizontal cells. Photoreceptors contain a light-absorbing visual pigment located in an area analogous to the dendrite. It is this pigment that initiates the neural reconstruction of the focused image. Photoreceptors appear in two forms: the

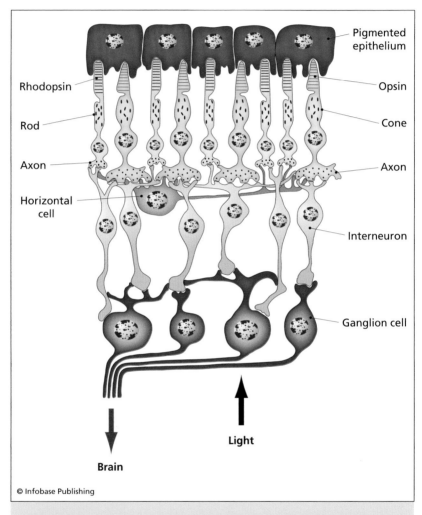

© Infobase Publishing

Retina. The photoreceptors (rods and cones) are embedded in pigmented epithelium at the back of the retina. Interneurons connect the photoreceptors to ganglion cells that send their axons to the visual cortex of the brain. Horizontal cells provide a lateral circuit that is used to enhance the contrast of the image before it is transmitted to the brain. The *RPE65* gene is expressed only in the cones.

rods, specialized for the reception of black-and-white images, and the cones, which can detect color. Signals from the photoreceptors are conveyed to the brain via the interneurons and ganglion cells. Axons from the ganglion cells are combined to form the optic nerve. The horizontal cells are used to process the image before it is sent on to the brain.

Rods have a visual pigment called rhodopsin. Each rod has 100 billion copies of this molecule, which allows the cell to detect a single photon. Rods cannot detect color, but their exquisite sensitivity makes them ideal for seeing at night or under low light conditions. Rods are not found in the fovea, so the image they produce has a low resolution. This is one of the reasons why it is difficult to read small print in dim light. More than 80 percent of the photoreceptors in the human eye are rods.

Cones have a special visual pigment called cone opsin that is adapted for color sensitivity and day vision. There are three different forms of this pigment, each adapted for the detection of a different color, which in the human eye are blue, green, and yellow. Cones are concentrated in the fovea and produce the sharpest image. It is for this reason that we must look straight at an object to get the clearest picture. The orientation of the cones and rods in the retina is in the opposite direction of the light pathway. This allows the retina to pull both of these photoreceptors deep into the pigmented epithelium at the back of the retina in order to guard against excessively bright light. This can occur, for example, when one leaves a movie theater on a bright sunny day. The initial fast response is a reduction in the pupil diameter to reduce the amount of light entering the eye. Within about 30 minutes, the retina will have pulled the photoreceptors into the pigmented epithelium, at which point the iris can reopen to its normal diameter.

The *RPE65* gene is expressed in retinal pigmented epithelium (the source of the gene's name) and in the cones. Recent studies have shown that RPE65 is a crucial enzyme, known as isomerohydrolase, that is involved in managing the biochemistry of light detection by the cones and is located in the membranes of those cells. RPE65 is a large protein containing 537 amino acids and its gene is located on chromosome 1. Two point mutations have been identified at positions 91 and 368. The mutation at position 91 converts an arginine to tryptophan, and the mutation at 368 converts a tyrosine to histidine. Scientists abbreviate these mutations as R91W and Y368H, using the single letter abbreviations for the amino acids as shown in the table on page 10. These mutations not only disrupt the normal function of this enzyme, but they apparently destroy the protein's membrane localization signal, for in all cases mutated Rpe65 is found in the cytoplasm instead of in the membrane of the cone cells.

The easy accessibility of the retina and the relatively uncomplicated nature of the mutations causing retinal dystrophy make this disease an ideal candidate for gene therapy. As discussed in chapter 9, a Phase I trial has currently concluded with very promising results.

3

Viruses: Cornerstones of Gene Therapy

Somebody once said that a virus is a piece of nucleic acid surrounded by bad news. When one thinks of all the trouble viruses have caused over the years, one can easily see the truth in it. Viruses have given us smallpox, polio, some forms of cancer, deadly influenza epidemics, the common cold, and the dreaded AIDS disease. And yet, for all of that, these masters of death and destruction are about to pay us back, in full and with interest. For without the viruses, there would be no gene therapy, and if one considers their ancestors, the plasmids, evolution of animal life on this planet would have been a much slower process.

When one speaks of curing someone of a genetic disease, one is referring to gene replacement, or the process of introducing a normal gene into a defective cell. But how is this to be done? Eukaryotes are a clever bunch, and they take a dim view of foreign genes dropping by for lunch. To protect their privacy, they have surrounded themselves with a membrane that blocks the passive entry of everything except the tiniest of molecules. Even if a piece of DNA could gain access to the cell, it would still have to get into the nucleus before it could be replicated and transcribed. But the nucleus, like the cell, is surrounded by a lipid bilayer that also prevents passive diffusion of anything larger than a water molecule.

These are only a few of the problems that viruses had to overcome as they evolved into cellular parasites. Their first task was to find a way to get their genome into a cell, so the cell's machinery could be used to reproduce their kind. How they managed this, and how their success has become essential for the success of gene therapy, is the subject of this chapter.

VIRUSES ARE LIVING CRYSTALS

Soon after James Watson and Francis Crick resolved the structure of DNA, Watson published a paper on viral structure in which he suggested that since a virus is such a tiny particle, less than one-tenth the size of a bacterium, it could only carry enough nucleic acid for a dozen or so genes. Consequently, he proposed viral structure must consist of only a few proteins, used over and over again in some sort of symmetrical, highly ordered arrangement. To test this idea, many biologists examined viral structure under the newly available electron microscope, and, when they did, they saw tiny crystalline structures that confirmed Watson's speculations.

Most viruses, including the herpes virus, adenovirus, and polio virus, have a crystalline protein structure that is icosahedral (constructed from triangles, like a geodesic dome). The protein crystal forms a hollow compartment, called the capsid, that contains the viral genome. In some cases, an envelope consisting of a lipid bilayer, which is often studded with proteins, surrounds the crystalline capsid. Some viruses, such as the influenza virus, have a simple, though highly ordered, spherical capsid instead of a crystalline icosahedron. The presence or absence of an envelope, the structure of the capsid, and the nature of the viral genome—that is, whether it is RNA or DNA—are the most important characteristics scientists use to identify and classify these organisms.

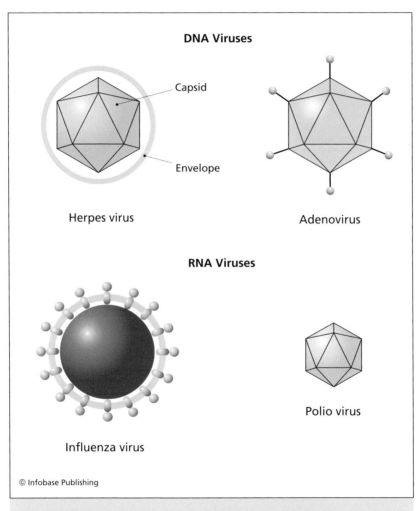

DNA Viruses

Capsid

Envelope

Herpes virus

Adenovirus

RNA Viruses

Influenza virus

Polio virus

© Infobase Publishing

Viral morphology. Herpes virus, adenovirus, and polio virus all have icosahedral capsids, or protein coats, that surround and protect the viral genome, which may be DNA or RNA. Herpes and influenza viruses are also surrounded by a lipid bilayer (envelope) that may be studded with proteins.

VIRAL GENOMES MAY BE RNA OR DNA

All cells, whether they are prokaryotes or eukaryotes, have DNA genomes. DNA is a very stable molecule that can store many thousands of genes, essential for the complex lifestyles of modern cells, which often have 20,000 to 30,000 genes. In addition, double-stranded DNA allows for error correction, an extremely important feature when millions of nucleotides are to be replicated.

Viruses, on the other hand, are extremely simple organisms, so simple that many of them get by with fewer than a dozen genes. When genomes are this small, the advantage of DNA over RNA disappears. Consequently, viruses come with many different kinds of genomes, some using DNA, others RNA. They may be single stranded or double stranded, circular or linear. Viruses with only a few genes have a single-stranded RNA genome, but as the number of genes increases the genome tends to be double-stranded DNA.

The adenovirus is a typical example of a DNA virus. This non-enveloped virus has a double-stranded DNA chromosome, containing 30 to 40 genes, that is capped at each end with a terminal protein offering added stability to the molecule. The capsid is constructed from repeating hexon and penton (six- or five-sided) proteins. A protein filament with a bulbous tip is attached to each penton and plays an important role in getting the virus inside a cell. Most of the remaining genes code for proteins that are needed for infection. A few of the genes code for histonelike proteins that bind to the chromosome for added stability. Adenoviruses, so named because they were originally isolated from the adenoid glands, cause the common cold and general infections of the upper respiratory tract.

The human immunodeficiency virus (HIV) is an example of an enveloped retrovirus that has an RNA genome. A retrovirus has a special enzyme called reverse transcriptase that converts the RNA chromosome to DNA after it infects a cell. This enzyme allows the virus to reverse the usual DNA to RNA direction of genetic biosynthesis and is the reason they are called retroviruses. The HIV capsid

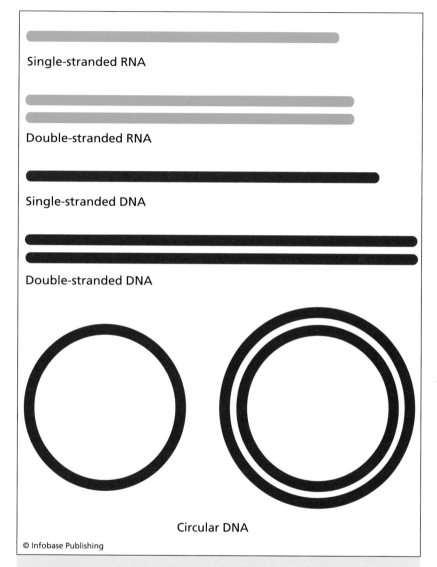

Single-stranded RNA

Double-stranded RNA

Single-stranded DNA

Double-stranded DNA

Circular DNA

© Infobase Publishing

Viral genomes. Small viruses with few genes have single-stranded RNA or DNA genomes. Large viruses with many genes (10 or more) always have double-stranded DNA genomes that are either linear or circular. In double-stranded genomes, one strand usually codes for all of the genes, while the second strand provides stability and error correction.

consists of a spherical protein matrix immediately beneath the envelope and a cone-shaped core that forms the genome compartment. The HIV genome consists of nine overlapping genes, three of which

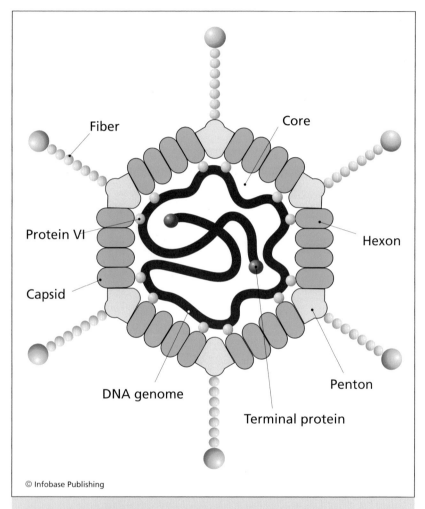

Fiber

Core

Protein VI

Hexon

Capsid

DNA genome

Penton

Terminal protein

© Infobase Publishing

Structure of the adenovirus. The capsid is constructed from repeating hexon and penton proteins. A long fibrous protein, attached to each penton, is crucial for cell entry. The DNA chromosome, anchored by protein VI, contains 30 to 40 genes and is stabilized by two terminal proteins. Several other proteins, not shown, are stored in the core to initiate and maintain infection.

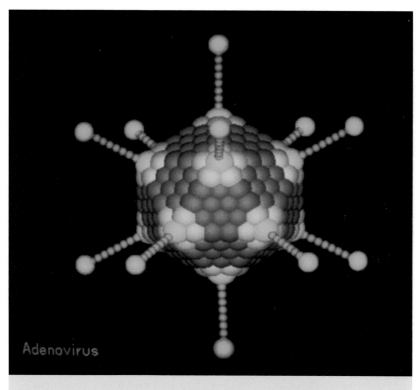

Adenovirus. *(Science Source/Photo Researchers, Inc.)*

(*Gag, Pol,* and *Env*) are common to all retroviruses. HIV belongs to a group of retroviruses known as lentiviruses and is responsible for the immune system disorder known as AIDS.

Overlapping genes are unique to viruses. In such a genome, one stretch of the chromosome can be used to code for two or three genes. Viruses also process their mRNA to produce more than one protein from any given gene. When this occurs, a precursor mRNA is synthesized from the gene, after which it is split in half to produce two different proteins. Consequently, the *Env* gene codes for two envelope proteins, glycoprotein (gp) 120 and 41 (the numbers refer to their relative sizes), and the *Gag* gene codes for the matrix (p17) and core (p24) proteins. In addition, genes for six regulatory proteins overlap the *Env* gene region of the chromosome. The *Pol*

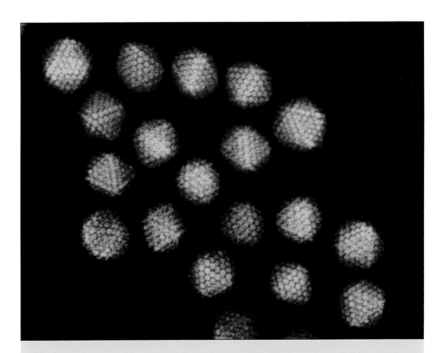

Transmission electron micrograph (TEM) showing a group of adenoviruses. There are 47 varieties of this virus worldwide, which attack the epithelial cells of the upper respiratory tract. In addition, some varieties are known to cause conjunctivitis of the eye and enteritis of the small intestine in toddlers and small children. Magnification: 200,000×. *(Eye of Science/Photo Researchers, Inc.)*

gene codes for reverse transcriptase. Despite their simple structure and small genome, retroviruses are the most virulent pathogens known. Aside from AIDS, they are responsible for several forms of cancer.

VIRUSES EVOLVED FROM PLASMIDS

It was once thought that because viruses are so simple, they must be extremely ancient and may have been the life-form that gave rise to the prokaryotes. But scientists have shown that all viruses are

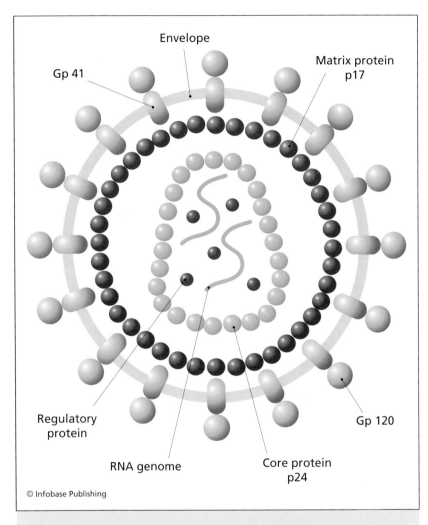

Structure of a retrovirus. The example, shown in cross section, is HIV, an enveloped retrovirus that has a double-stranded RNA genome containing nine genes. The capsid consists of a spherical matrix and an inner, cone-shaped protein core. Glycoproteins (Gp) 41 and 120, embedded in the envelope, are crucial for cell entry. Several regulatory proteins, including reverse transcriptase, are stored in the core.

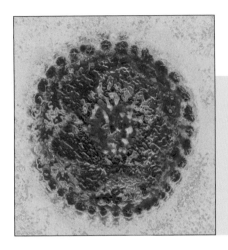

Avian influenza, a virus of the Orthomyxoviridae family. This flu virus causes an infectious and contagious respiratory disease and often results in a pandemic and/or smaller seasonal epidemics. *(James Cavallini/Photo Researchers, Inc.)*

cellular parasites, incapable of replicating their genome or of synthesizing their proteins without using cellular machinery. Consequently, they must have evolved after cells appeared, and their most likely ancestors are bacterial plasmids.

Plasmids are mini-chromosomes that bacteria have been swapping among themselves for more than a billion years. This form of prehistoric neighborly behavior was often of mutual benefit. Plasmids carry antibiotic-resistance genes, so if a cell happens to make one that is particularly good, another, unrelated bacterium could get a copy simply by capturing the plasmid. Plasmids were probably released into the environment when a cell's membrane became leaky, for various reasons, or when the cell died and broke open, an event that echoes the molecular sharing that may have occurred among the prebiotic bubbles that gave rise to the first living cells. But plasmid exchange among prokaryotes could only work as long as the plasmids stayed small enough to reenter an intact cell by passive diffusion.

The first virus was probably a plasmid that picked up a gene for a protein that could spontaneously form a capsid. Acquiring a capsid made it possible for the virus to interact with cell-surface receptors, some of which are like doorways into the cell, so the virus was no longer dependent on passive diffusion for entry. In this sense, acquiring a capsid was like finding the key to the cell's door. Once the cell-surface barrier was removed, the viral genome was free to increase in size from a few genes to a few dozen. With a larger genome, viruses evolved a wide range of strategies for entering cells and, once inside, taking over cellular machinery to suit their own purposes.

VIRUSES KNOW HOW TO INFECT CELLS

All cells need to communicate with the outside world, and in particular they need a system for detecting and collecting food molecules. Prokaryotes satisfied these requirements by embedding protein receptors in their cell membrane. These receptors are part of a grander structure called the glycocalyx, a molecular forest that covers the cell membrane, reminiscent of the forests that once covered the surface of the Earth. With the establishment of the glycocalyx, the cell membrane became increasingly resistant to the passive diffusion of large molecules. That is, it tended not to leak as much as it did in primitive cells. This trend, begun by the prokaryotes, was converted to a rule by the eukaryotes: Anything coming in has to pass a port of entry.

Ports of entry include sugar receptors, hormone receptors, and ion channels. Ion channels are usually open, permitting free access to the cell's interior, but the pore size is small enough to block entry to large molecules and microbes. The sugar receptors and some hormone receptors are linked to a process called endocytosis that is able to bring large molecules and microbes into the cell. When the proper molecule makes contact with these receptors, they are drawn inside by the formation of a vesicle (bubble). This type of entry is called receptor-mediated endocytosis.

Viral capsids can activate endocytosis to gain entry into a cell. Once inside, the virus releases an enzyme that attacks the

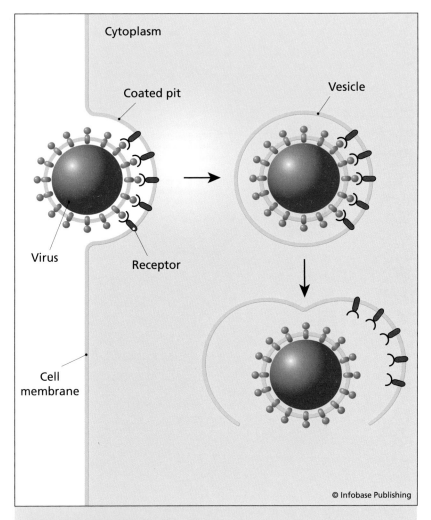

Receptor-mediated endocytosis. A virus enters a cell by binding to receptors in a coated pit, which activates endocytosis, a process the cell normally uses to ingest food or signal molecules. Once inside, a viral enzyme attacks the wall of the vesicle, causing it to rupture, releasing the virus into the cytoplasm.

wall of the vesicle, causing it to rupture, thus releasing the viral capsid into the cytoplasm. There are several variations to this scheme. For example, the AIDS virus binds to cell receptors but does not activate endocytosis. Instead, the viral envelope fuses with the cell membrane, releasing the capsid directly into the cytoplasm without the formation of a vesicle. In all cases, once the capsid is free in the cytoplasm, it breaks open to release the viral chromosome.

When an adenovirus enters a cell, the partially fragmented capsid binds to a nuclear pore, after which the chromosome moves into the nucleus, where it is replicated and transcribed. Viral mRNA and copies of its genome then move from the nucleus to the cytoplasm where the mRNA is translated into capsid and other viral proteins. The replicated genome and the newly synthesized viral proteins auto-assemble into mature viral particles, which leave the cell by rupturing the cell membrane, killing the cell in the process.

The life cycle of a retrovirus is more complex than that of an adenovirus. When a retrovirus infects a cell, the capsid core breaks open to release the RNA genome into the cytoplasm, which is quickly converted to DNA by reverse transcriptase. The viral DNA moves into the nucleus and inserts itself into one of the cell's chromosomes. After insertion, the viral genes are transcribed, producing mRNA, and the entire length of viral DNA is transcribed to produce many copies of the viral RNA chromosome. The mRNA and the RNA chromosomes migrate back to the cytoplasm where the mRNA is translated into capsid, regulatory, and envelope proteins, the latter of which are sent to the cell membrane by way of the endoplasmic reticulum and Golgi complex.

New capsids form by the auto-assembly of the newly made RNA chromosomes and capsid proteins. The cell membrane, now studded with viral proteins, then forms an envelope around the viral particles as they leave the cell in a process called exocytosis. Thus, the lipid bilayer that surrounds this type of virus is obtained from the cell, while the envelope proteins are of viral origin. An important feature of this life cycle is that the virus does not rupture the membrane and hence does not kill the cell when it leaves.

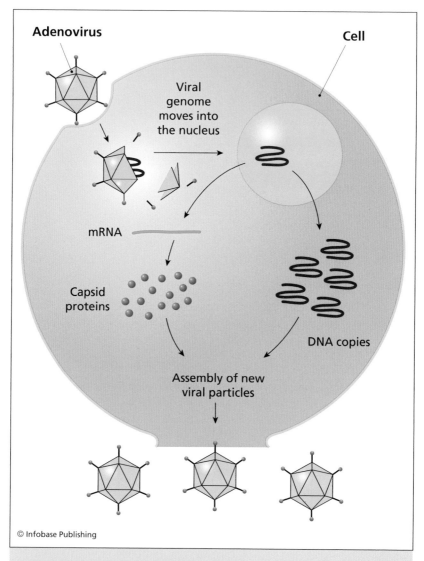

Adenovirus

Cell

Viral
genome
moves into
the nucleus

mRNA

Capsid
proteins

DNA copies

Assembly of new
viral particles

© Infobase Publishing

Life cycle of an adenovirus. After the virus enters the cell, the fragmented capsid docks at a nuclear pore (not shown) and releases the chromosome into the nucleus, where it is replicated and transcribed. The replicated DNA and the mRNA leave the nucleus and enter the cytoplasm. The viral mRNA is translated in the cytoplasm, and the proteins join with the DNA copies to form new viral particles, which leave the cell by disrupting the membrane.

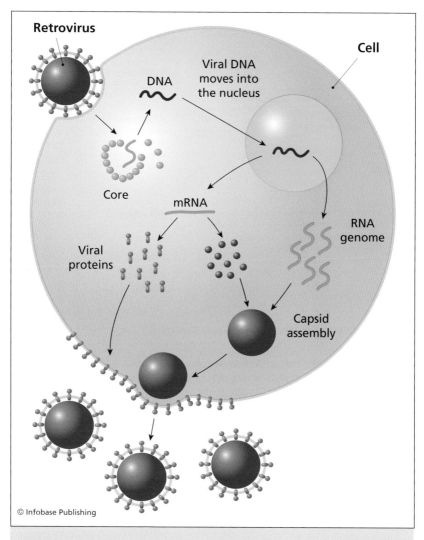

Retrovirus

Cell

Viral DNA
moves into
the nucleus

DNA

Core

mRNA

RNA
genome

Viral
proteins

Capsid
assembly

© Infobase Publishing

Life cycle of a retrovirus. After the virus enters the cell, the RNA chromosome is released from the core and copied into DNA by reverse transcriptase. The DNA chromosome enters the nucleus, where it integrates into a host chromosome, after which it is transcribed into RNA. The RNA leaves the nucleus, some of which is translated into capsid and envelope proteins, and the rest becomes new copies of the RNA genome. The translated viral proteins are embedded in the membrane. The assembled capsid obtains an envelope made of cell membrane and retroviral proteins while leaving the cell by exocytosis.

Colored transmission electron micrograph (TEM) of HIV viruses budding from an infected T lymphocyte human blood cell (the cell is at bottom [pink]). HIV (human immunodeficiency virus) causes AIDS. Four viruses are seen in different stages of budding: at center left, the virus acquires its coat from the cell membrane (red); at right, the virus buds from the cell; at center right, budding is almost complete; at left, the new virus is free-floating. Once free, the HIV virus with central RNA (green) reinfects other T cells. T cells form part of the body's immune response and are weakened by the HIV virus. Magnification: 86,000×. *(NIBSC/Photo Researchers, Inc.)*

THE VIRUS AS A GENE VEHICLE

Given their talents for entering cells, viruses would appear to be ideal candidates for gene delivery vehicles or vectors. But there are two major problems to overcome before they can be used safely: First, the ability of the virus to replicate its own genome must be blocked, along with the production of viral mRNA that codes for proteins that maintain the infection and help the virus escape from the cell. Second, the therapeutic gene has to be inserted into the viral genome in such a way that it will not inhibit the formation of a normal capsid, since this is the part of the virus that is essential for cell entry.

Production of viral gene vehicles is carried out in a test tube. Viral genes needed for replication and the maintenance of infection are removed, after which the therapeutic gene is inserted into the viral chromosome. The hybrid chromosome is added to a test tube and mixed with purified viral capsid proteins, leading to the auto-assembly of viral particles. If this is done properly, the virus will be able to enter the cell to deliver the gene, but it will not harm the cell or be able to reproduce itself.

VIRUSES USED IN GENE THERAPY

Adenovirus type 2 (AD-2) and a retrovirus called murine (mouse) leukemia virus (MLV) have been used in more than 90 percent of all gene therapy trials to date. AD-2, although naturally adapted to infecting the upper respiratory tract, has been used in trials that targeted T lymphocytes, liver, skin, and a variety of tumor cells. An important consideration when using this virus is the amount to give the patient. In a trial attempting to treat a liver ailment, for example, the recombinant AD-2 is injected directly into that organ. If the number of viral particles injected is correct, the liver receptors will bind up all of the viral particles. If the amount is too low, too few cells will take up the virus, so expression of the therapeutic gene will be insufficient to treat, or cure, the disease. If the amount is too high, viral particles will spill out into the general circulation and infect a variety of cells. Being crippled, these viruses cannot damage the cells they infect, but their presence can lead to a potentially deadly immune response as T cells detect and destroy infected cells. In extreme cases, this can lead to the destruction of entire organs and death of the patient.

While the adenovirus has proved to be a good delivery vehicle, the expression of the therapeutic gene tends to decline after a week or two. This is believed to be due to the extra chromosomal life cycle of this virus. That is, the viral chromosome enters the cell nucleus, but it does not integrate into a host chromosome. Under these conditions, the cell's machinery does not continue transcribing the therapeutic gene. Moreover, AD vectors are inefficient at infecting some cells, and they tend to activate an antivector immune response.

Consequently, most clinical trials use a retrovirus as a delivery vehicle. Indeed, the retrovirus is not only the current favorite but was the first to be developed for gene therapy. These viruses are very efficient at infecting cells of the immune system (the AIDS virus has made that clear) and they do not elicit as strong an immune response as do other vectors. Moreover, the retroviral life cycle includes integration of its genome into the host chromosome. Once it is in the chromosome, the therapeutic gene is expressed at a steady rate.

Unfortunately, in many cases, the rate at which a therapeutic gene is expressed by a retroviral vector is too low to cure the patient or even to alleviate some of the symptoms. In addition, there is always some apprehension about using an integrating virus, because if something goes wrong, there is, at present, no way to get it out again. This is particularly worrisome, since in an attempt to increase expression of the therapeutic gene some gene therapy trials use retroviral vectors that are replication competent (can still reproduce).

The justification for designing replication-competent retroviral vectors is that these viruses do not kill the cell when they exit. If its pathology-inducing genes are removed, reproduction of the vector and its movement from cell to cell are of no concern. Vector reproduction leads to an increased number of cells being infected and thus increases the amount of therapeutic protein being synthesized, with subsequent benefits for the patient. However, there is always the possibility that one of these vectors will encounter another virus infecting the patient and, through genetic recombination, become pathogenic and possibly deadly.

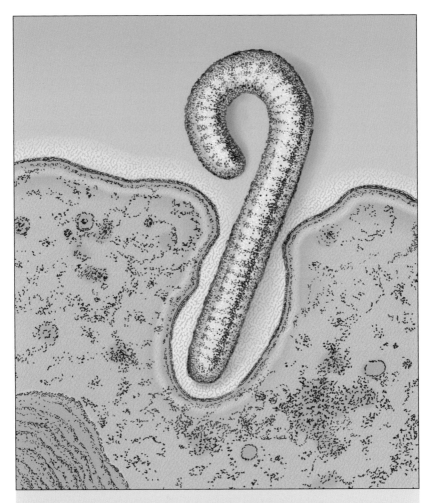

Ebola virus infecting a human liver cell via endocytosis. The virus was named after a river in the Democratic Republic of the Congo where it was first discovered in 1976. It is an RNA virus of the family Filoviridae known to cause the often-fatal disease Ebola hemorrhagic fever (EHF). *(Chris Bjornberg/Photo Researchers, Inc.)*

An alternative approach involves genetic engineering of hybrid retroviruses that might produce large quantities of the therapeutic protein, while being unable to replicate. To this end, scientists have created an Ebola-HIV viral hybrid to be used as a novel gene-delivery vehicle. Scientists know that both viruses are deadly and exceptionally talented when it comes to infecting cells. The hybrid appears to work well in animal experimentation, but whether it will ever be approved for use in human gene therapy trials is another question. The scare factor associated with a vector like this is such that many people will be reluctant to have it injected into their veins.

VIRAL ECOLOGY

Viruses, like bacteria, seem to be everywhere. Indeed, a recent estimate of the number of viruses in marine ecosystems has shown that they outnumber bacteria by a wide margin. Scientists believe that there are thousands of viral species, most of which have yet to be identified. Viruses infect all living things from bacteria to mammals, but as is the case with bacteria not all of them are pathogenic. In general, viruses are host-specific; that is, there are viruses that specialize in infecting bacteria, while others only infect plants, or protozoans, or animals. Viruses may also specialize within a taxonomic group. For example, bird viruses and tiger viruses usually do not infect humans. Scientists believe the first viruses appeared on Earth more than 3 billion years ago making them almost as ancient as the first cells.

Although viruses were introduced at the beginning of this chapter as being living crystals, the question as to whether they are alive or not is controversial. Many scientists believe that viruses occupy a gray zone between the living and the nonliving. This idea has persisted for so long that a serious study of viral ecology has only been possible in recent years. Scientists who believe viruses are not truly alive argue that they simply acquire lifelike properties from their hosts, most notably their ability to reproduce and their highly organized structure. By extending this argument, one could assume that if all bacteria, plants, and animals disappeared suddenly from the face of the Earth, viruses would soon follow. On the other hand, if all the viruses disappeared, everything else would continue on as though nothing had happened.

Those who believe viruses are alive counter that the above argument does not apply because it is true of all parasites. Much of the controversy has focused on the apparent simplicity of viruses, and many critics believe that such simple structures cannot really be alive. But the largest known virus, the mimivirus that infects amoebae, is almost as complex as the simplest bacterium. Part of the problem may be that the definition of life is too rigid. As the British playwright George Bernard Shaw once wrote, "You think that life is nothing but not being stone dead."

In any event, genomic studies suggest that, dead or alive, viruses have played an important role in the evolution of life on Earth. Two examples of viral influence on evolution, the role of jumping genes in forming the structure of the eukaryote genome and the horizontal transfer of genes, were discussed in chapter 1. In addition, viruses may have played a direct role in the evolution of eukaryotes (protozoans and the cells of plants and animals) from the prokaryotes (bacteria and their ancestors). Dr. Luis Villarreal, director of the Center for Virus Research at the University of California, Irvine, has suggested that the cell nucleus, which typifies eukaryotes, may have evolved from a persistent viral infection of an ancient population of prokaryotes. Consequently, had viruses disappeared millions of years ago, everything else would not have continued on as though nothing had happened. Indeed, eukaryotes might not have appeared at all.

Ashi DeSilva:
A Promising Start

Michael Blaese, W. French Anderson, and their associates at the National Institutes of Health (NIH) conducted the first gene therapy trial in 1990. There were only two patients in that trial: Ashi DeSilva who was then just four years old and Cynthia Cutshall who was nine years old. Cutshall showed only modest improvements following the treatment, but for DeSilva it was a dramatic success.

Both patients suffered from a genetic disease called severe combined immunodeficiency (SCID), briefly described in chapter 2. SCID is an immune system disorder that makes it very difficult for those afflicted to fight off even mild diseases, such as the common cold or influenza. The term *combined immunodeficiency* refers to the involvement of both the T and B lymphocytes. The term *severe* was used in the original descriptions of this disease because most children had a severe clinical disease and died before their second birthday. However, by the time DeSilva was treated, diagnosis and

National Institutes of Health (NIH). This view of NIH's campus looks north past the Natcher Building (right) to the Stokes Labs (center) and beyond to the Clinical Center (upper left). Building 31, the Claude D. Pepper Building (upper right), provides office space for most institute directors and their immediate staff. *(NIH Almanac)*

improved treatments (other than gene therapy) meant that most children lived much longer. Today, severe refers more to the lifestyle that SCID patients have to endure than an early death.

The particular form of SCID that DeSilva and Cutshall suffered from was due to a deficiency in an enzyme called adenosine deaminase (ADA). The gene for this enzyme is located on the long arm of chromosome 20. Humans, being diploid creatures, receive a copy of each chromosome from both parents; this is nature's way of protecting us from genetic abnormalities. A child who receives a defective ADA gene from one parent and a healthy ADA gene from the other parent will not develop SCID because the defective gene is recessive to the normal gene. That is, the normal gene makes a functional copy of the protein, thus compensating for the defective copy made

The first gene therapy patients—
11-year-old Cynthia Cutshall
(at left) and six-year-old Ashi
DeSilva *(Ted Thai/Time Life Pictures/Getty Images)*

by the mutated gene. This is why ADA deficiency is referred to as an autosomal recessive genetic defect and why genetic diseases, in general, are rare. Symptoms occur only if the child receives defective ADA genes from both parents.

DeSilva and Cutshall were admitted to the trial in the hope that gene therapy would cure their disease. Both patients responded well to the treatment, but, as the reader will see, the trial itself was the tip of a scientific iceberg, resting on top of a mountain of preliminary research stretching back to the early 1970s. This work included the identification of ADA as the source of the clinical symptoms, isolation of the ADA gene, and years of work that clarified the role of this gene and how the genetic defect led to a crippled immune system. Preliminary research was also concerned with the details of the gene therapy procedure: the type of virus used as the gene vehicle, the joining of the isolated ADA gene to the virus, and the method used to deliver the ADA-virus construct to the patient. These things all had to be worked out in detail using animal models before gene therapy could be used to treat a human patient.

ADENOSINE DEAMINASE

ADA is an enzyme involved in the purine salvage pathway. Purines, such as adenine and guanine, are structural components of nucleotides. The cell recycles these molecules continuously, using them to construct new nucleotides, fats, or proteins. Decomposition of a nucleotide begins with the removal of the phosphates by a nucleotidase and the removal of an amino group on the purine by ADA. The molecule that is left behind, called inosine, is broken down further by other enzymes. Inosine components, the free phosphates, and the amino group are all recycled. In the absence of ADA, adenosine concentrations build up to toxic levels, damaging both the B and T lymphocytes and impeding their replication, thus making it impossible for them to mount an effective immune response.

CELLS OF THE IMMUNE SYSTEM

The human immune system is composed of a diverse group of white blood cells that are divided into three major categories: granulocytes, monocytes, and lymphocytes. Granulocytes have a distinctive, lobular nucleus, and all are phagocytic. Lymphocytes have a smooth morphology and a large, round nucleus. T lymphocytes and natural killer (NK) cells deal primarily with coordinating the immune response and killing already-infected body cells. B lymphocytes are nonphagocytic; they deal with an invading microbe by releasing antibodies. Monocytes are large phagocytic cells that look very much like free-living amoeba. The largest monocytes, the macrophages, can engulf whole bacteria as well as damaged, or senescent, body cells.

Phagocytosis of an invading microbe by granulocytes and monocytes represents a first-line defense, called the innate response. All animals are capable of mounting this kind of defense. Activation of the lymphocytes leads to a more powerful second line of defense, called the adaptive response, which is found only in higher vertebrates and is initiated by the monocytes. These cells,

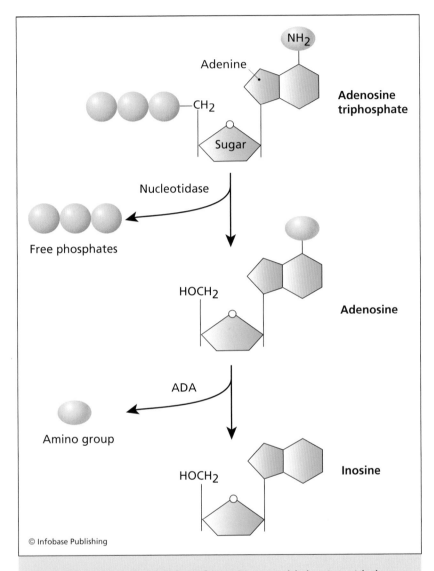

Recycling adenosine triphosphate. Disassembly begins with the removal of the phosphates by a nucleotidase to produce the nucleoside adenosine, followed by the removal of the amino group by adenosine deaminase (ADA) to produce inosine. All three components are recycled to make new nucleotides and amino acids.

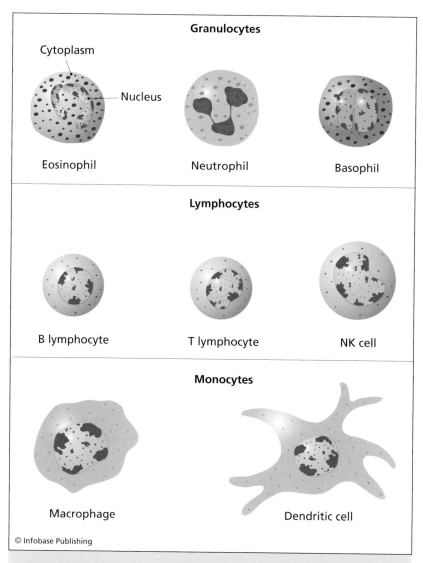

Granulocytes

Cytoplasm

Nucleus

Eosinophil   Neutrophil   Basophil

Lymphocytes

B lymphocyte   T lymphocyte   NK cell

Monocytes

Macrophage   Dendritic cell

© Infobase Publishing

White blood cells. These cells are divided into three major categories: granulocytes, lymphocytes, and monocytes. Granulocytes have a distinctive lobular nucleus, granulated cytoplasm, and all are phagocytic (eat cells, viruses, and debris). Lymphocytes have a smooth morphology with a large round or kidney-shaped nucleus. B lymphocytes are nonphagocytic but produce antibodies. T lymphocytes and natural killer (NK) cells coordinate the immune response and can force infected cells to commit suicide. Monocytes are large cells with an irregular shape. All monocytes are phagocytic and large enough to engulf whole bacteria and damaged or senescent body cells.

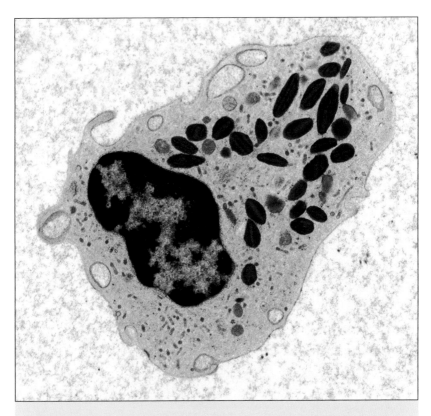

White blood cell. Colored transmission electron micrograph (TEM) of an eosinophil (white blood cell), part of the body's immune system. The cell's nucleus (black) contains chromatin (green). In the cell's cytoplasm (yellow) are many enzyme-containing granules (purple), used to destroy invading organisms. Eosinophils are involved in the body's allergic response and also help to defend the body from invading parasites. They are capable of ingesting and destroying foreign particles by a process known as phagocytosis. Magnification: 5,000×. *(Steve Gschmeissner/Photo Researchers, Inc.)*

after engulfing a virus or bacterium, literally tear the microbe apart and then embed the pieces, now called antigens, in their membrane. The antigens are presented to lymphocytes, which become activated when their receptors bind to the microbial antigens. Activated B lymphocytes secrete antibodies specifically designed to combat that particular microbe. Activated T cells and NK cells attack the mi-

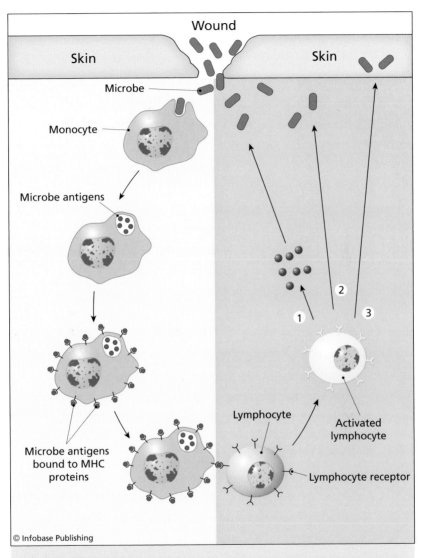

Innate and adaptive immune response. Phagocytosis of invading microbes is called the innate response (yellow zone). In higher vertebrates, microbe antigens, bound to special monocyte surface proteins called the major histocompatibility complex (MHC), are then presented to lymphocytes. Contact between the lymphocyte receptor and the antigen activates the lymphocyte and the adaptive response (blue zone), consisting of a three-pronged attack: 1) release of antibodies, which kill the microbes; 2) direct attack on the microbes; 3) destruction of infected cells.

crobe directly but are primarily concerned with locating and killing infected body cells.

The adaptive system can remember a pathogen long after it has been removed from the body. This is why a specific bacteria or virus strain cannot make us sick twice. Once infected, humans develop a natural, lifelong immunity. Physicians use a crippled version of a pathogen, or specific antigens from a pathogen, to immunize the general public against specific diseases. This concoction of bits and pieces from a pathogen, called an immunizing serum, will activate the adaptive response, giving a lasting, though not always lifelong, immunity to the disease. The adaptive system, consisting of activated B and T lymphocytes, is extremely powerful, and it is this system that is destroyed by adenosine deaminase deficiency, for the lack of this enzyme cripples both the B and T lymphocytes.

The activities of a healthy immune system, particularly the function of T lymphocytes and NK cells, have a direct bearing on the outcome of a gene therapy trial. The immune system will attack and destroy anything that is foreign and that includes a viral vector carrying a therapeutic gene. Were it not for this problem, gene therapy would be relatively straightforward procedure.

PRELIMINARY RESEARCH

Studies involving ADA and its role in SCID can be traced back to the 1970s. These very early studies were concerned with the identification of the defective enzyme and which cells of the immune system were affected. Between 1972 and 1978, ADA was identified as the enzyme responsible for the disease, and a buildup of adenosine was shown to be specifically toxic to T and B lymphocytes.

The ADA gene was isolated and sequenced in 1985, and several mutations were identified by 1989. Over this same time period, methods were being developed to treat ADA deficiency with bone marrow transplants and infusions of PEG-ADA, the drug that temporarily supplies copies of ADA. Both of these procedures help some patients but each comes with its own set of problems and disadvantages. The major problem associated with transplants is finding a suitable donor. Even if such a donor is found, there is still the possibility the transplant will be rejected or will cause serious side effects.

PEG-ADA is a drug that is produced by linking ADA to a molecule called polyethylene glycol (PEG), which increases its stability in the patient's bloodstream. Pure ADA has a half-life of only 30 minutes to one hour, while PEG-ADA can last for up to two to three days. The drug has to be injected directly into the bloodstream, meaning that young children must be subjected to an unpleasant procedure every other day for all of their lives. Moreover, as already noted, the drug does not cure the disease, and children receiving the drug are still incapable of mounting an effective immune response to a variety of diseases.

To deal with the shortcomings of the standard treatment, Blaese and his team began to explore the possibility of treating ADA deficiency with gene therapy as early as 1987 when they submitted their first proposal for a Phase I trial to NIH Recombinant DNA Advisory Committee (RAC) based on preclinical results from monkeys. The review process, then as now, was extremely rigorous. The proposal was reviewed by at least a dozen scientists who made recommendations, which had to be addressed before RAC would approve the trial. Among the recommendations were three primary concerns that RAC had regarding the safety of the procedure:

1. The number of transduced cells (cells infected with the vector-ADA gene) obtained in monkey gene-transfer models was very low, and there was no evidence that totipotent stem cells, the optimal target cells, had been transduced.

2. Even though the ADA gene was expressed efficiently in mature ADA-deficient T cells in tissue culture,

there was no evidence that the gene would remain active during the differentiation of T cell precursors to the final mature T cell found in general circulation.

3. The ADA vector preparation available at that time was contaminated with a helper virus (a virus that helps insert the ADA gene into the vector), and there were only preliminary in vivo primate data (obtained from monkeys) suggesting that a helper virus might not pose a public health risk.

These questions, together with the success of PEG-ADA treatment and the fact that the protocol called for the treatment of infants, led the RAC to conclude that additional work was needed to confirm the safety of the virus and the protocol in adult subjects, before it could be used to treat infants or children. Accordingly, Blaese was given permission in 1989 to conduct a Phase I clinical trial using adult human cancer patients. The basic layout of the procedure included the following: lymphocytes, isolated from the patients, were transformed with retrovirus and then returned to the donor patient. Adults were used in this trial because the dangers could be fully explained to them so the requirements regarding informed consent were met.

The trial was intended to confirm the safety of the vector and the infusion procedure in human subjects, both of which had been tested extensively in mice and rhesus monkeys that had received infusions of ADA transgenic lymphocytes. As an added precaution, the vector used in the human cancer trial did not carry a therapeutic gene, but it did carry the marker sequence *NeoR,* so the investigators could follow the fate of the vector and proliferation of the infused cells. They found that the *NeoR* gene remained active for up to five months.

The information collected in the cancer trial suggested that a therapeutic gene would remain active for long periods and could be expected to improve the clinical symptoms of a disease such as ADA deficiency. In addition, none of the six trial patients experienced abnormalities, side effects, toxicities, or pathology due to the retroviral-mediated gene-transfer procedure, thus confirming the earlier results with mice and monkeys. Based on these results, the RAC gave formal approval for a Phase I trial to treat ADA deficiency in children.

UNDERSTANDING CLINICAL TRIALS

Clinical trials are conducted in four phases and are always preceded by experiments conducted on animals such as mice, rats, or monkeys. The format for preclinical research is informal. It is conducted in a variety of research labs around the world, and the results are published in scientific journals. Formal approval from a governmental regulatory body is not required.

Phase I Clinical Trial

Pending the outcome of the preclinical research, investigators may apply for permission to try the experiments on human subjects. Applications in the United States are made to the Food and Drug Administration (FDA), the NIH, and the RAC. The RAC was set up by the NIH to monitor any research, including clinical trials, dealing with cloning, recombinant DNA, or gene therapy. Phase I trials are conducted on a small number of adult volunteers, usually between two and 20, who have given informed consent. That is, the investigators explain the procedure, the possible outcomes, and, especially, the dangers associated with the procedure before the subjects sign a consent form. The purpose of the Phase I trial is to determine the overall effect the treatment has on humans. A treatment that works well in monkeys or mice may not work at all on humans. Similarly, a treatment that appears safe in lab animals may be toxic, even deadly, when given to humans. Since most clinical trials are testing a new drug of some kind, the first priority is to determine a safe dosage for humans. Consequently, subjects in the Phase I trial are given a range of doses, all of which, even the high dose, are less than the highest dose given to experimental animals. If the results from the Phase I trial are promising, the investigators may apply for permission to proceed to Phase II.

Phase II Clinical Trial

Having established the general protocol, or procedure, the investigators now try to replicate the encouraging results from Phase I, but with a much larger number of subjects (100–300). Only with a large number of subjects is it possible to prove the treatment has an effect. In addition, dangerous side effects may have been missed in Phase I because of a small sample size. The results from Phase II will determine how safe the procedure is and whether it works or not. If the statistics show the treatment is effective and toxicity is low, the investigators may apply for permission to proceed to Phase III.

Phase III Clinical Trial

Based on Phase II results the procedure may look very promising, but before it can be used as a routine treatment it must be tested on thousands of patients at a variety of research centers. This is the expensive part of bringing a new drug or therapy to market, costing millions, sometimes billions, of dollars. It is for this reason that Phase III clinical trials invariably have the financial backing of large pharmaceutical or biotechnology companies. If the results of the Phase II trial are confirmed in Phase III, the FDA will approve the use of the drug for routine treatment. The use of the drug or treatment now passes into an informal Phase IV trial.

Phase IV Clinical Trial

Even though the treatment has gained formal approval, its performance is monitored for very long-term effects, sometimes stretching on for 10 to 20 years. In this way, the FDA retains the power to recall the drug long after it has become a part of standard medical procedure. It can happen that in the long term, the drug costs more than an alternative, in which case, health insurance providers may refuse to cover the cost of the treatment.

MEDICAL PROCEDURE FOR ADA GENE THERAPY

The standard treatment for ADA deficiency is a bone marrow transplant or a drug, called PEG-ADA that supplies normal copies of the enzyme to the patient. Bone marrow transplants were not possible for DeSilva or Cutshall owing to the lack of compatible donors. Both patients were being treated with PEG-ADA in the months leading up to the trial. Indeed, this treatment was a requirement for entry into the trial, as it improved their health, which would be beneficial in the event of any side effects due to the trial. Although PEG-ADA relieves many of the symptoms of this disease, it is not a cure. The drug provides an extracellular source of normal ADA, but the internal environments of each B and T lymphocyte are still deficient. Consequently, even with ADA supplements, the immune system does not function normally.

The procedure for ADA gene therapy begins with the removal of some T lymphocytes from patients being treated with PEG-ADA. The T cells are grown in tissue culture, and a normal ADA gene is inserted into them using a process called retroviral-mediated gene transfer, after which the gene-corrected, or transgenic, cells are returned to the patient. The vector is a modified murine leukemia virus (retrovirus), called LASN, into which the ADA gene has been inserted.

The protocol was designed to have two parts. In part one, low numbers of gene-corrected T lymphocytes were given to the patient repeatedly in order to build up the immune system and also to obtain information as to how long gene-corrected T cells survive. In part two A, a selection procedure was used to increase the number of gene-corrected T cells making substantial amounts of the ADA enzyme. These enriched cells were then given to the patient monthly for approximately six months. In part two B, the number of gene-corrected T cells were increased to the predicted therapeutic level (about 1 billion gene-corrected T cells per kilogram body weight of the patient). Then, 1 billion to 3 billion gene-corrected T cells per kilogram (2.2 lbs) were infused several times, after which the patient was monitored in order to determine if the immune system was functioning normally.

THE DESILVA CLINICAL TRIAL

On September 14, 1990, Ashi DeSilva became one of two patients enrolled in the first-ever gene therapy trial. Cynthia Cutshall joined the trial on January 31, 1991. Anderson and Blaese led the trial, which involved a total of 30 principal investigators and nursing personnel. DeSilva's lymphocytes were isolated, grown in culture, and transduced with the LASN vector containing the ADA gene, as already described. Almost from the first day of the trial her immune response improved. Transfusions were continued for two years, after which her response to the trial was closely monitored. Both patients showed an improvement, but DeSilva's response exceeded everyone's expectations. Within five to six months of beginning the trial, DeSilva's T cell count rapidly increased and stabilized in the normal range. ADA enzyme activity, nearly undetectable in her lymphocytes initially, increased in concentration during the first two years of treatment, reaching a level roughly half that of a normal value. This may seem inadequate, but it was enough for her to lead a normal life. A detailed account of the trial was published in the journal *Science*.

DeSilva's immune response has diminished somewhat since the trial, but it currently remains within the normal range, and she no longer requires a regular infusion of transgenic T cells. Cutshall did not respond as well to the treatment, but she has shown a gradual increase in the proportion of functional transgenic T cells and like DeSilva enjoys a normal lifestyle.

The reduction in DeSilva's immune response may be due to an autoimmune response that is leading to the destruction of some of her own T lymphocytes. This can happen if monocytes encounter vector antigens and present them to T lymphocytes, thus activating an adaptive response against the vector and any cells containing it. In this particular case, the autoimmune response would be mild, since the retrovirus generally remains in the nucleus thus minimizing exposure of its antigens.

The DeSilva trial proved that gene therapy can be used to cure certain genetic diseases. Interest in the procedure increased dramatically from only a few trials in the early 1990s to more than 1,500 trials worldwide in 2009. Most of these trials are designed to treat various forms of cancer, but a few are attempting to cure SCID by combining gene therapy with stem cell therapy. Italian, British, and French medical teams, using transgenic stem cells, have reported complete success in curing patients suffering from SCID-ADA and SCID-X1, an interleukin-deficient form of SCID. (See chapter 9 for more information.) These teams have all used improved versions of the LASN vector that Blaese and his colleagues developed. This, coupled with the use of transgenic stem cells, has greatly improved the percentage of successful outcomes. In this approach, isolated stem cells are transfected with the therapeutic gene and then injected into the patient where they differentiate into mature T lymphocytes possessing improved functionality. In the British trial, for example, eight out of nine patients showed dramatic improvements in the function of their immune response. However, all of these trials are still at the Phase II or III level and have yet to be approved as a standard therapy.

5

Jesse Gelsinger:
The First Fatality

Throughout the 1990s, the gene therapy community was riding a wave of euphoria brought on by the great success of the DeSilva trial. Even though there were some in the science community who complained that gene therapy promised more than it could deliver, most observers were impressed with the accomplishments and the potential benefits such a procedure could bring to medical practice.

Critics, however, pointed out that the performance of gene therapy between 1990 and 1998 was of little consequence. Several trials had been launched to cure other patients of SCID-ADA without success, reducing the initial success rate to one in 20. Even so, the potential for gene therapy continued to be held in high regard, and the number of trials increased from one in 1990 to more than 300 in 1998. Most scientists were not concerned with the low success rate. They realized that with such a novel and complex therapy, it could take several decades before the wrinkles were ironed out of the protocols. In addition, there was general agreement that the DeSilva trial had made the crucial point: Gene therapy works. It is only a matter of time before the procedure is refined enough that it will work for everyone.

It was during this euphoric period in 1995 that the University of Pennsylvania set up its Institute for Human Gene Therapy (IHGT) and hired Dr. Jim Wilson as its director. Wilson, in turn, hired Dr. Mark Batshaw, a physician long interested in gene therapy who had devised one of the first drugs to treat ornithine transcarbamylase (OTC) deficiency, a genetic disease that affects the liver. Batshaw convinced Wilson to make OTC deficiency the subject of their first gene therapy trial, and they began by studying the properties of various viruses that might serve as gene therapy vectors. Rather than use the LASN vector or another retrovirus, they decided to use an adenovirus (AD virus), because in animal models it seemed

Sculpture of Benjamin Franklin at the University of Pennsylvania by John Boyle in 1899. *(Alamy Images)*

Jesse Gelsinger. *(Paul Gelsinger)*

to be a more efficient vector. In 1997, after a year spent working out the details of their procedure, they applied for and were granted permission to conduct a Phase I gene therapy trial to correct OTC deficiency in adult patients.

The trial began in fall 1998 with 18 patients enrolled. The 18th patient and, at age 18, the youngest to volunteer was Jesse Gelsinger. The trial was terminated a year later, just four days after Gelsinger was treated. On the second day of his treatment, Gelsinger lapsed into a coma and 24 hours later was pronounced dead. Within days of Gelsinger's death, NIH ordered a halt to all AD-vector gene therapy trials being conducted in the United States. The ban lasted a full year and was accompanied by an investigation that was not concluded until fall 2001. Gene therapy was placed on trial, certainly the most rigorous trial any medical procedure has ever had to endure. For a time it looked as though Gelsinger's death was also the death of a promising therapy and Wilson and Batshaw's careers.

ORNITHINE TRANSCARBAMYLASE

OTC is a liver enzyme that rids the body of toxic ammonia, which is generated when our cells recycle protein. The first step in the recycling process liberates free amino acids; the second step involves the release of an amino group (NH_2), found on every amino acid. The amino group is quickly converted to ammonia (NH_3 or NH_4)

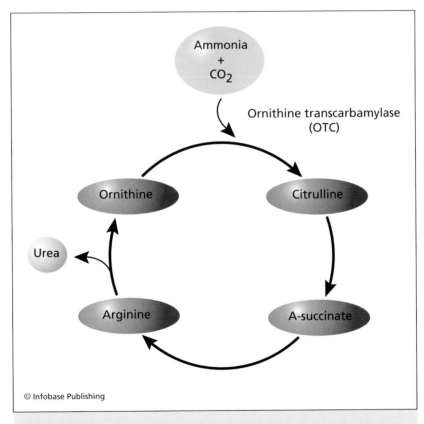

© Infobase Publishing

Urea cycle. Cells in the liver rid the body of toxic ammonia by converting it to urea, which is then excreted by the kidneys as urine. Ammonia and carbon dioxide (CO_2) are added to ornithine to produce citrulline, a reaction that is catalyzed by the enzyme OTC. Other enzymes in the cycle produce argininosuccinate (A-succinate) and arginine; the latter is split into urea and ornithine, thus completing the cycle.

with the addition of one or two hydrogen atoms. The ammonia is ultimately converted to urea by the liver in a series of biochemical reactions known as the urea cycle. The kidneys readily excrete urea in the urine, from which urine gets its name.

Ammonia enters the urea cycle when it, along with carbon dioxide (CO_2), is added to ornithine to produce citrulline; OTC catalyzes this crucial step in the cycle. When OTC is defective, ammonia levels build up in the blood, resulting in convulsions, vomiting, and coma, with death following quickly if treatment is not administered. The central nervous system is especially vulnerable to ammonia levels, because neurons, being extremely energetic, require a constant supply of adenosine triphosphate (ATP) (the molecule that all cells use as the ultimate source of energy). Ammonia blocks the production of ATP, leading quickly to the death of neurons and other especially active cells, such as muscle cells and cells of the digestive tract. Convulsions and vomiting are early signs of energy-starved muscle and intestinal cells.

PRELIMINARY RESEARCH

Ammonia intoxication, referred to as hyperammonemic syndrome (or hyperammonemia), was described in the early 1960s and quickly connected to a defect in the urea cycle. The urea cycle is a series of biochemical reactions that was discovered by Hans Krebs and Kurt Henseleit in 1932, five years before Krebs described the many reactions involved in the citric acid cycle.

The urea cycle was the first cyclic metabolic pathway to be discovered. It consists of five enzymes, defects in any one of which can cripple the liver's ability to produce urea. Mutations have been described for all of the urea cycle enzymes, but throughout the 1980s it became clear that OTC deficiency was by far the most common mutation, accounting for more than 40 percent of all mutations affecting urea production. It is also the most lethal. Patients suffering from mutations in other urea cycle enzymes, leading to a buildup of citrulline or arginine, for example, are easily treated and rarely suffer the life-threatening coma that is associated with increased ammonia concentrations in the blood.

OTC deficiency, and the study of it, brings us around to the grand ecological association between animals, plants, and prokaryotes, all focused on the use of nitrogenous compounds and the problems organisms have when trying to recycle them. Ammonia and amino acids, both nitrogenous compounds, were produced in the stormy environment of prebiotic Earth. When the first cells appeared, they found themselves in an environment rich in these compounds. Amino acids could be used directly to form simple proteins, and, as the original supply of amino acids was depleted, cells learned how to manufacture their own amino acids by using ammonia from the atmosphere. Eventually, the atmospheric ammonia was depleted (something one is grateful for now), but by that time prokaryotes and certain plants had evolved that could capture molecular nitrogen from the atmosphere, a process called nitrogen fixation. By capturing nitrogen from the atmosphere, these organisms ensured a ready supply of nitrogenous compounds for all living things in the ecosystem.

There is, of course, a limited amount of nitrogen in our ecosystem; plants return theirs when they die and decompose. Animals likewise return nitrogen to the ecosystem when they die, but they also return a great deal of it throughout their lives as urine. Animals produce the urine by way of recycling amino acids, and when they do it is as though they are resurrecting the Earth's ancient, ammonia-rich atmosphere. Because of its toxicity, early cells quickly learned to convert the free ammonia to urea, thus giving birth to the urea cycle.

Genetic defects affecting the urea cycle in general and OTC in particular are fairly common, affecting one in 20,000 male children every year in the United States alone. Consequently, the hunt for the OTC gene began almost as soon as recombinant DNA technology made the effort a possibility. By 1989, the gene for OTC had been isolated, several mutations described in detail, and its location on the X chromosome confirmed. The OTC gene, because of its location, is referred to as being X-linked, and as a consequence the most serious cases are always among males, who have a single X chromosome, in contrast to females who have two. Women are usually asymptomatic carriers but do occasionally suffer a mild form of the disease owing to the random inactivation of one of their X chromosomes (for genetic stability, human females, like their male counterparts, have one functional X chromosome per cell). Mild forms of OTC deficiency can occur in males as the result of a random mutation that damages the OTC gene in some, but not all, liver cells, thus producing a somatic cell mosaic for the OTC gene (some cells in the liver are normal, while some are defective). This is the form of the disease that Jesse Gelsinger suffered from, and it is generally referred to as a partial deficiency of OTC.

MEDICAL PROCEDURE FOR OTC GENE THERAPY

There are substantial differences between OTC gene therapy and the procedure described for ADA deficiency. OTC is not located in single blood-borne cells as is ADA. Instead, this particular genetic abnormality affects an organ. Consequently, it is not practical to collect a few liver cells, transfect them with the corrected gene, and then return them to the body (although this may be possible with stem cells). Instead, OTC gene therapy involves the injection of the viral vector into the blood, or directly into the liver, which it is hoped will transfect liver cells, thus curing, or at least treating, the disease.

Another difference is that OTC gene therapy is administered using an adenovirus (AD virus) rather than a retrovirus, as is used to treat ADA deficiencies. The AD virus causes upper respiratory tract infections, the common cold, and conjunctivitis (eye infection), all of which are usually mild infections. Gene therapists believe that the AD virus is a more potent vector in that it supports expression of the transgene (in this case, the OTC gene) at therapeutic levels. That is, the amount of OTC produced will either cure the disease or result in an obvious reduction of the clinical symptoms.

After OTC patients are injected with the virus, they must be carefully monitored for toxic side effects of the treatment and for any improvement in ammonia metabolism. Toxicity is evaluated by determining the biochemical behavior of the liver, blood concentrations of ammonia and urea, urine output, and general kidney function. The patients' white blood cell count, which serves as an indicator of immune response, is also determined. Potential risks that gene therapists prepare for include direct or immune-mediated injuries to the liver, kidneys, heart, and lungs.

Wilson's team at the University of Pennsylvania Hospital developed a protocol for their first gene therapy trial in which an AD vector was to be administered to 18 patients by direct infusion into the right hepatic (liver) artery. Delivery rates and volume of instillation were to be kept constant for all participants. Cohorts of three subjects would be assigned to six dosing regimens, with each cohort receiving a progressively higher dose of vector, adjusted for the body weight of each subject. The first two participants in each cohort were to be females, with male subjects only eligible as the third subject in each cohort. Doses ranged from 1.4×10^{11} (140 billion) vector particles to 3.8×10^{13} (38 trillion) virus particles. The vector was to be administered to the cohorts in tandem; that is, cohort 1 would be dosed and monitored before treatment began on cohort 2. (This is the reason the trial had been under way a full year before Gelsinger was treated.) Within each cohort, the female subjects would receive the virus before the males. Dosing the patients in this way made it possible to incorporate several stopping rules. For example, if cohort 1 suffered toxic side effects, either cohort 2 would not be treated or it would be treated with a lower dose. If the female subjects within any cohort suffered severe side effects, the male would not be treated. The rationale for this stopping rule is that the female carriers of OTC deficiency, being heterozygous, are generally in better health than symptomatic males and thus better able to deal with toxic side effects.

THE GELSINGER CLINICAL TRIAL

On September 9, 1999, Jesse Gelsinger caught a flight from his home in Arizona to Philadelphia, Pennsylvania. His father, Paul Gelsinger, was to join him shortly after the trial began. On Monday morning, September 13, Gelsinger checked into the hospital at the University of Pennsylvania and was taken to the interventional-radiology suite where he was sedated and a catheter was passed into his liver from a vein in his groin. At 10:30 A.M., the attending surgeon, Dr. Steve Raper, attached a syringe to the catheter and slowly injected 30 ml (about 1 ounce) of an AD vector carrying the OTC gene.

Gelsinger was the second patient in cohort 6, receiving the highest dose of 38 trillion vector particles. Injecting the vector directly into the liver was thought to be safer than injecting it into general circulation. If the treatment went as planned, liver receptors would bind all of the viral particles, thus minimizing the exposure of the rest of the body to the vector. Infusion of the vector was complete by 12:30 P.M. That night, Gelsinger developed a fever and became sick to his stomach, an expected early reaction. By early Tuesday morning, however, his condition became serious. He was disoriented and the whites of his eyes had turned yellow, an early sign of liver damage and possible onset of a clotting disorder called disseminated intravascular coagulation (DIC).

The normal daily turnover of red blood cells (RBCs) is the link between yellowing eyes and liver damage. When RBCs are recycled, a major breakdown product is a yellowish compound called bilirubin, which is normally broken down by the liver. If the liver is damaged, the concentration of bilirubin in the blood increases very quickly, thus affecting the color of the eyes. The destruction of RBCs can be unnaturally high in a patient suffering from DIC, which accelerates the rate at which bilirubin accumulates. DIC is a complex syndrome that is usually triggered by a massive bacterial or viral infection and is initiated by monocytes as part of the innate immune response. Serious trouble begins with the activation of the adaptive system. Because the infection is so severe, T lymphocytes and NK cells begin killing large numbers of infected cells, so many, in fact, that it inflicts serious damage to entire organs. Complicating matters, the T lymphocytes release an enormous number of communication molecules, called interleukins, to maximize the extent of the adaptive response. The high concentration of interleukins, however, stimulates inappropriate coagulation of the blood throughout the circulatory system. The systemwide formation of blood clots blocks the flow of blood through the capillaries, thus depriving tissues of nutrients and oxygen. The end result, in Gelsinger's case, was tissue swelling and multi-organ failure.

The problem of DIC is compounded in a patient suffering from OTC deficiency, because the blood clots weaken the liver still further, leading to a rapid increase in plasma levels of ammonia. Moreover, the only treatment for DIC is to deal with the underlying cause, the microbial infection. In Gelsinger's case, the infecting agent, the AD vector, was overpowering and impossible to treat directly. By Tuesday afternoon, Gelsinger had slipped into a coma and was placed on blood dialysis to control the ammonia concentration that was rising to dangerous levels. Paul Gelsinger arrived at the hospital early Wednesday morning, and Raper and Batshaw told him they would have to put his son into a deeper coma in order to control the rising level of ammonia in his blood. Later that afternoon, Gelsinger's lungs and kidneys began to fail and his body and face swelled to such an extent that he was barely recognizable. On Friday morning, September 17, Jesse Gelsinger was declared brain-dead, and he died 2:30 P.M. that day.

THE INVESTIGATION

Wilson reported Gelsinger's death immediately. Officials at FDA and NIH decided to terminate all AD vector gene therapy trials pending a full review of Gelsinger's case. A preliminary review was conducted from November 30, 1999, to January 19, 2000. The full review was to last for more than a year and covered every aspect of Wilson's protocol and the criteria used to admit patients to the trial. The investigation also examined the research labs at Genovo, a biotechnology company founded by Dr. Wilson, because it was there that much of the preclinical research was carried out. Genovo was also funding one-fifth of the operating budget for the IHGT, established by Wilson at the University of Pennsylvania, and in return Genovo had exclusive rights to patent and market any of IHGT's discoveries.

In January 2000, NIH released preliminary results of their investigation, which cited Wilson and Batshaw for failure to adhere to the clinical protocol and an apparent disregard for the safety of the study subjects. The report focused on the following four main points.

1. **Failure to adhere to the stopping rules.** Toxic reactions observed in cohorts 1 to 5 should have led to termination of the trial long before Gelsinger was treated. Many of the patients in these groups suffered harsher reactions to the treatment than was expected, and this should have been sufficient reason to stop the trial. In addition, most of the toxic reactions experienced by the patients in this study had never been reported to FDA or NIH. In the months following Gelsinger's death, other investigations showed that failure to report toxic reactions was common in many gene therapy trials. In one study, the patients experienced 691 serious side effects, of which only 39 were reported as required by the federal agencies.

2. **Failure to adhere to the principle of informed consent.** When a toxic response occurred in cohort 1 of the Gelsinger trial, cohort 2 should have been informed of this response to give those patients the option of withdrawing from the study. This was not done. Moreover, the investigators discovered that none of the subjects were told about adverse affects on monkeys in the preclinical trial. One of the monkeys received the same virus used in the clinical trial, though at a higher dose, and within a week of being treated it was euthanized because it developed the same clotting disorder that killed Gelsinger. Since none of the subjects were told about this, the consent forms were ruled invalid.

3. **Failure to keep adequate records regarding vector lineage and titer.** This was an especially damaging finding since it implied that the researchers gave Gelsinger more virus than they thought they had. The term *titer* refers to the number of vector particles in a given solution. Determining the titer is not straightforward, and if errors are made the concentration may be incorrect by a factor of 10, rather than double, or triple the amount expected. The possibility that Gelsinger was accidentally given a higher-than-stated dose is suggested by the fact that a woman in his cohort received a nearly identical dose (38 trillion vector particles) without signs of liver damage or DIC. As already mentioned, a monkey in a preclinical trial received a higher dose (17 times greater) of the same virus and subsequently developed DIC. If researchers made an error in calculating the dose for Gelsinger, it is possible he received an equivalent, fatal amount.

4. **Changing the protocol without approval.** The most serious infraction here had to do with the ammonia

levels in the blood of prospective volunteers. As laid out in the original protocol, patients having more than 50 micromoles of ammonia per milliliter of blood were barred from volunteering because such a test result indicates severe liver damage. (This concentration is roughly equivalent to a pinch of salt in a gallon of water.) Sometime after the trial, however, researchers increased this maximum to 70 micromoles without formal approval from the FDA. Gelsinger's ammonia level, on the day he was treated, was about 60 micromoles. If the original cutoff had been adhered to, he would have been excluded from the study. In fairness to Wilson's team, it should be noted that ammonia levels fluctuate on a daily basis, and previous tests of Gelsinger's blood showed it to be below 50 micromoles.

CONCLUSIONS

The death of Jesse Gelsinger had the same effect on the gene therapy community that the *Challenger* (1986) and *Columbia* (2003) space shuttle disasters had on NASA's space program. The initial shock and trauma associated with the destruction of the shuttles was followed by a determined and unrelenting investigation that clarified the many events leading up to the accidents and, at the same time, produced a clear picture of what had to be done to ensure that such terrible accidents never happen again.

Many things were changed at NASA to help shake the program administrators out of their complacency and to open their eyes to the real dangers of each space shuttle mission. Similarly, the gene therapy community had begun to think the procedure was so safe and straightforward that they were lulled into complacency, and in the case of the OTC trial researchers ignored warning signs that could have prevented both Gelsinger's death and the severe illnesses other members of the trial developed.

In March 2000, after the completion of their investigation of the Gelsinger trial, the FDA and NIH announced a set of new initiatives to protect participants in gene therapy trials. The main thrust of the new guidelines is a monitoring plan that requires strict adherence on the part of the investigators to report within seven days any and all toxic affects. All such reports are now reviewed by an independent data and safety monitoring board before the trial is allowed to continue. To ensure compliance, NIH investigators now make frequent and unannounced visits to the institutions where gene therapy trials are being conducted. The new initiatives also require full disclosure of preclinical data to potential volunteers before they sign the consent form. Consistent with this goal is a new database at the NIH Web site that provides public access to detailed information concerning NIH-funded gene therapy trials. The FDA has established a similar public access point for this kind of information with its gene therapy patient tracking system, established in June 2002 and made available on their Web site. In that same year, Paul Gelsinger joined a human rights organization called Citizens for Responsible Care and Research (CIRCARE) that is dedicated to the protection of human subjects in research and medical treatment (discussed further in chapter 8).

Even in the darkest hours immediately following the death of Jesse Gelsinger, no one believed it would be the end of gene therapy, any more than the destruction of the space shuttles was thought to signal the end of the space program. In the case of gene therapy, science offers cures for a wide variety of noxious diseases that have plagued humans for centuries. With the new regulations in place and safer procedures being developed, scientists will continue their efforts to realize its full potential.

6

Future Prospects

Gene therapy has had its ups and downs. Indeed, more than any other new biology technology, this one is the most erratic. There was great success with the DeSilva case but a terrible failure with the Gelsinger case. A more recent trial to cure SCIDs, led by Dr. Alain Fischer and initially thought to be the most successful ever, began having trouble when four of the participants developed a vector-induced leukemia. (See chapter 9 for details.)

The problems encountered by the Fischer trial have helped scientists define what must be resolved in order to improve the safety of this procedure. Safer vehicles must be found or designed, strategies must be developed to minimize immune rejection of the vector, and greater emphasis must be placed on risk assessment. The last of these three problem areas will be relatively easy to achieve, but the first two represent profoundly difficult biological problems that are likely to take many years to resolve.

SAFER VEHICLES

A safe vehicle is one that enters only the target cells and inserts itself into a safe location within the genome—that is, well away from any genes. Retroviruses, for reasons outlined in chapter 3, are the vector of choice for most gene therapy trials, but none of them are capable of this kind of specificity. The failure of the Fischer trial, which used a modified retrovirus (MLV), occurred because the vector inserted itself into a stretch of DNA in or near a gene called *LMO2* that is known to be involved in cancer induction, particularly leukemias.

Scientists have estimated that the MLV vector used in the Fischer trial could have inserted itself in the *LMO2* gene in 1 in 100,000 cells. Each patient in the trial received about 1 million genetically modified cells, so it is likely that some of the patients received at least one cell containing a vector-mutated *LMO2* gene. However, this estimate is based on the assumption that vector insertion is random, which may not always be the case. Some viruses may insert themselves nonrandomly into preferred sites within the genome. In this way, a leukemia virus, such as MLV, may habitually insert itself in or near genes that cause cancer, in which case the number of cells damaged in the Fischer trial may have been much higher than 1 in 100,000. Consequently, a virus such as MLV may never be a safe vehicle. Nonrandom insertion poses a serious threat to virus-based gene therapy, but it also suggests a way of improving the safety of all insertional vectors, for if they are nonrandom, there may be a way of designing a vector that will only insert itself into specific areas of the genome.

Sequence-Specific Vector Insertion

A viral protein called an integrase regulates insertion of viral DNA into the chromosome. During the life cycle of a retrovirus the conversion of the RNA genome into DNA is followed by the translocation of the viral DNA into the cell's nucleus, where it is transcribed

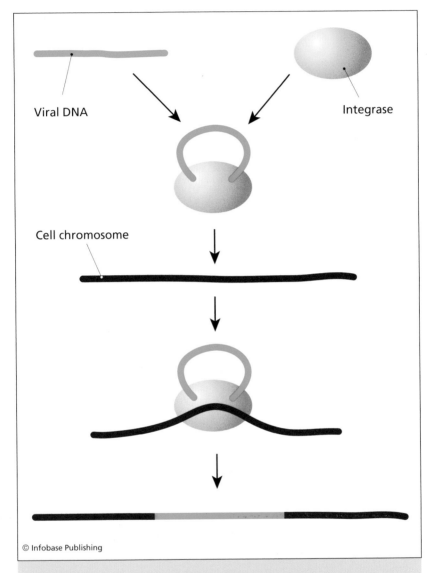

Viral DNA

Integrase

Cell chromosome

© Infobase Publishing

Integration of viral DNA into a cellular chromosome. The protein integrase binds to the viral DNA and then to the cellular chromosome (target), after which it cuts the target chromosome in a single place and inserts the viral DNA. Final sealing of the target and viral DNA is left to the cell's repair enzymes (not shown). The length of the viral DNA, relative to the cell chromosome, is exaggerated for clarity.

into messenger RNAs (mRNAs). The viral mRNAs move out to the cytoplasm where they are translated into protein. Integrase is among this group of viral proteins; because it carries a nuclear localization signal, cellular enzymes escort it back into the nucleus, where it catalyzes the insertion of viral DNA into host chromosomes. The details of this event involve the binding of the integrase to the viral DNA, cutting of the host DNA by the integrase, and, finally, insertion of the viral DNA into the cell's chromosome.

Thus, it is the integrase that decides where the viral DNA will be inserted. It is this protein and others like it that will make sequence-specific insertion possible. With the complete nucleotide sequence of the human genome now at hand, scientists will be able to map out the exact location of all human genes and the noncoding regions. Careful analysis of this data will make it possible to design a family of integrase molecules that will place a vector in a noncoding region of the genome. Indeed, it may be possible to map out entire genetic neighborhoods that could be designated as safe insertional sites, that all gene therapists could use without fear of damaging cellular genes. This approach will give gene therapy the kind of rational foundation that it lacks today.

Improved Targeting of Cells and Organs

The most successful gene therapy trial to date is still the very first one: the DeSilva trial. The success of this trial is largely due to the fact that the target cells were lymphocytes, cells that could be easily isolated and removed from the blood, transformed with the corrected gene, and then returned to the patient's circulatory system. There is no targeting problem here, and while other things can still go wrong, as the Fischer trial demonstrated, the gene therapists know that the vector carrying the therapeutic gene is restricted to a single cell type.

This was not the case with the Gelsinger trial. Liver cells cannot be harvested, transformed, and then returned to the patient.

Instead, the vector had to be injected into the body, after which the physicians crossed their fingers and hoped that most of it ended up in liver cells and not everywhere else in the body. The scientists conducting the Gelsinger trial took special precautions to ensure that the vector remained in the liver, but it did not. The virus spilled out into general circulation where it entered many different kinds of cells throughout Gelsinger's body, with disastrous consequences. But if a vector is safe and designed to insert itself away from cellular genes, does it really matter if it enters a single cell type versus many? Were it not for the patient's immune system, the answer to this question would be no. But the immune system will try to kill any cells that are infected with the vector. The infected cell, in effect, signs it own death warrant by displaying vector antigens on its surface. Lymphocytes detect these foreign antigens and either kill the cell directly or force it to commit suicide. This system is essential for fighting infectious diseases, but it does not understand the difference between a gene therapy vector and an influenza virus. Consequently, gene therapy must be designed to minimize the number of cell types that will become infected with the vector. If the vector does stimulate an immune response, then physicians only have to deal with the possible failure of a single organ versus the multiorgan failure that killed Jesse Gelsinger.

Improved targeting requires matching either viral capsid proteins, such as the adenovirus fiber proteins (seen on page 56) or the retroviral gp120 (seen on page 59) to cell-surface receptors. A hypothetical matching scheme, using a retrovirus, is shown in the figure on page 107. Accomplishing such a matching scheme will be extremely difficult, as it requires detailed sequence information for both the viral proteins and the cell surface receptors. Some of this information is currently available for the vectors, and with the human genome sequence data now available reliable targeting will likely be available for gene therapy trials in the next 10 years.

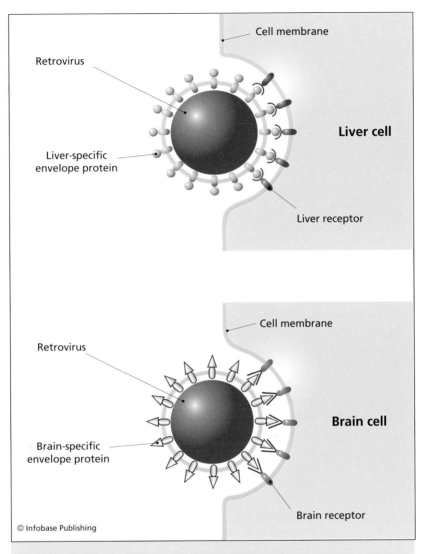

Vector targeting for safer gene therapy. Greater safety can be achieved by designing vectors that have cell-specific envelope proteins. In this way, for instance, brain-specific vectors would not be able to enter liver cells and liver-specific vectors would be blocked from entering brain cells.

REDUCING IMMUNE REJECTION OF THE VECTOR

Gene therapy trials that target the cells of solid organs require injection of the vehicle into general circulation. This is analogous to throwing a sheep into a den of very hungry wolves. Immune system sentinels begin an immediate attack on the invader, and their pursuit is relentless. Most of the vector particles will never make it to the target cells, and those that do may end up being destroyed by natural killer cells along with any cells they have entered. It is not surprising, therefore, that the efficiency of gene therapy is extremely low, often too low to be therapeutic. Thus, gene therapists face challenges that are identical to those arising from organ transplantations. Both have to negotiate with the patient's immune system, or there is no hope of success. For gene therapists, as for transplant surgeons, there are only two ways to deal with the immune system: Give the patient immunosuppressants to deactivate the system, or camouflage the vector in some way to make it invisible, or at least acceptable, to the lymphocytes and other members of the immune system.

Immunosuppressants

Two drugs commonly used for organ transplants are cyclosporine and tacrolimus. Both of these compounds are isolated from fungus and exert their effect by blocking the adaptive immune response, thus inactivating recruitment of T lymphocytes and natural killer cells by the monocytes. One or both of these drugs could be given to a patient immediately before the vector is administered and then slowly withdrawn once it has entered the target cells. However, to date, immunosuppressants have not been used but are under study for inclusion in future gene therapy trials.

Vector Camouflage

Artificial vectors consisting of a phospholipid sphere called a liposome have been designed in the hope of camouflaging the vector from the immune system. The immune system is on guard against

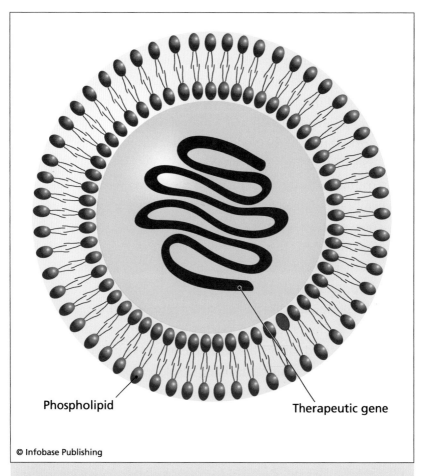

Phospholipid   Therapeutic gene

Lipid vectors. Artificial vectors can be made for gene therapy by en-casing the therapeutic gene inside a bubble called a liposome. These vectors are made by trapping a small drop of liquid containing the therapeutic gene within a phospholipid bilayer. Lipid vectors have the advantage of not being attacked by the immune system. On the other hand, they lack targeting specificity and will enter virtually ev-ery cell in the body.

foreign glycoproteins and glycolipids, because these macromol-ecules are components of the glycocalyx, the molecular forest that covers the surface of every cell. From the lymphocyte's point of view, evaluating a glycocalyx is rather like being an ecologist flying over a forest on Earth and getting a general impression of the forest's identity and health by noting the kind and variety of trees that are present. In this sense, a forest on Earth is an ecological fingerprint. In the world of immunology, the glycocalyx is a cellular fingerprint. Lymphocytes are programmed to know which fingerprints represent a normal part of the body; those that fail to register as self are marked as foreign and dealt with accordingly.

Phospholipids, the base material for prokaryote and eukaryote cell membranes, are not deemed to be a threat by the immune system; consequently, a liposome can move through the circulatory system unmolested. The great disadvantage of lipid vectors is their lack of target specificity. A liposome can readily diffuse across any cell membrane and, if there are enough of them, will enter every cell in the body. As explained, a viral vector entering most or all of the cells in the body can lead to a fatal multiorgan failure when the immune system destroys the infected cells. With liposomes, there is no danger of viral antigens being displayed on the membrane of infected cells, but the lack of targeting specificity is a problem for other reasons. First, the therapeutic gene will be expressed in nontarget cells. Disregarding the wastefulness of this result, there is no telling what effect the gene may have in an inappropriate cellular environment. Second, since the vector is entering many cells, its effects on the target cells will be diluted and therefore diminished. Gene therapists try to maximize the amount of the therapeutic gene that enters the target cells so the therapy has a chance of doing some good. Gene therapy trials often fail because too little of the vector gets into too few of the target cells. Although the gene is expressed in those cells, it often is not enough to relieve the patient's symptoms.

Nevertheless, lipid vectors have great potential, and it may be possible to improve targeting specificity by embedding proteins in the bilayer that will bind to cell-specific receptors, while at the same time being acceptable to the immune system. Most of the work with lipid vectors is at the initial stage of development, being tested primarily in mice and rats. Routine use of these vectors in human trials is not expected for many years.

IMPROVED RISK ASSESSMENT

In their report following the death of Jesse Gelsinger, the National Institutes of Health (NIH) focused extensively on the issue of risk assessment, particularly regarding the detection and reporting of toxic reactions experienced by the patients in the Gelsinger clinical trial. NIH investigators noted that most of the toxic reactions experienced by the patients in that study were never reported to the Food and Drug Administration (FDA) or NIH, and that follow-up investigations concluded that failure to report toxic reactions was common in many gene therapy trials. In one study (cited in chapter 5), the patients experienced 691 serious side effects, of which only 39 were reported as required by the federal agencies.

Legal guidelines are now in place to force investigators to report toxic reactions. (However, as discussed in chapter 8, these guidelines are difficult to enforce.) The problem lies in determining the parameters that are to be tested and the cutoff point that separates a benign response from a toxic reaction. Important elements of good risk assessment include the following: initial vector titer and subsequent vector concentration in the patients' blood, vector insertion and proliferation, and the response status of the immune system. Jesse Gelsinger may have died simply because the initial vector titer (the number of viral particles per milliliter) of the solution injected into his liver was too high. Obvious errors such as this occur more frequently than scientists like to admit but can be minimized by a three-tiered evaluation protocol (three independent determinations of the titer).

Future vectors will be designed to insert at specific places within the genome. But a vector designed for improved targeting cannot be trusted to do what it is programmed to do. Tests must be incorporated into a standard gene therapy protocol that determine the actual insertion site of the vector, and, if it is not where it is supposed to be, steps must be taken to deal with the possible side effects. These evaluations pertain to any evidence that suggests the virus is replicating. Most viruses used for gene therapy are altered so they cannot replicate, but it is always possible that the vector will encounter a wild virus, already infecting the patient, and that the two will recombine genetically to produce a replication-competent vector. Research is also under way to improve targeting of cells and organs. Clinical trials must include tests to confirm the targeting of these vectors, and, if vectors enter a variety of nontarget cells, such information should be taken as an alarm to prepare for a possible toxic response.

The final area of risk assessment, involving the immune system response, is the easiest to evaluate and yet provides the most important information. It was, after all, the response of Gelsinger's immune system that proved fatal. An increasing white blood cell count following vector administration coupled with high vector titer is a deadly mix and needs to be the focus of any attempt to improve the safety of gene therapy.

REDESIGNING HUMANS

With the human genome now completely sequenced and researchers actively seeking ways to move genes in and out of cell nuclei, it will soon be possible to modify our physiology, not just for the purpose of fighting disease but in an attempt to change the way the body functions and even to change the way it looks. These applications are fundamentally different from attempts to correct a medical disorder in that they could change human nature rather than reestablishing normal functions. Indeed, once gene therapy matures, there will be no limit to the kinds of things that it can do to our cellular and physiological systems. The possibilities may be grouped into three kinds of gene therapy: physiological, cosmetic, and bizarre. Ethical and legal questions regarding the future applications of gene therapy will be left to following chapters.

Physiological Gene Therapy

It takes more than carbon-based organic compounds to run a human being. Inorganic salts such as sodium chloride, potassium chloride, and calcium chloride play important roles in our physiology. Metals such as iron and copper also have a role to play. Indeed, without these metals, one would suffocate for lack of oxygen or fall into a deep coma for lack of ATP, the energy carrier that is vital to the survival of every cell in the body. ATP is produced by mitochondria in a two-step process involving a number of metal-binding proteins called the respiratory chain (also known as the electron transport chain) and a special ion channel enzyme called ATP synthase. The respiratory chain consists of three major components: NADH dehydrogenase, cytochrome b, and cytochrome oxidase. All of these components are protein complexes that have an iron (in the case of NADH dehydrogenase and cytochrome b) or a copper core (cytochrome oxidase). These components, along with the ATP synthase, are located in the inner membrane of the mitochondria.

The respiratory chain is analogous to an electric cable that transports electricity from a hydroelectric dam to our homes, where it is used to turn on lights or to run a stereo. Humans, like all animals, generate electricity by processing food molecules through a metabolic pathway called the Krebs cycle. The electricity, or electrons so generated, are not released as free particles but are transferred to a hydrogen ion (H^+), which quickly binds to nicotinamide adenine dinucleotide (NAD). Binding of the hydrogen ion to NAD is noted by adding an "H" to the acronym (NADH). The electrons begin their journey down the respiratory chain when NADH binds to NADH dehydrogenase, the first component in the chain. This enzyme does just what its name implies: It removes the hydrogen from NADH, releasing the stored electrons, which are conducted through the

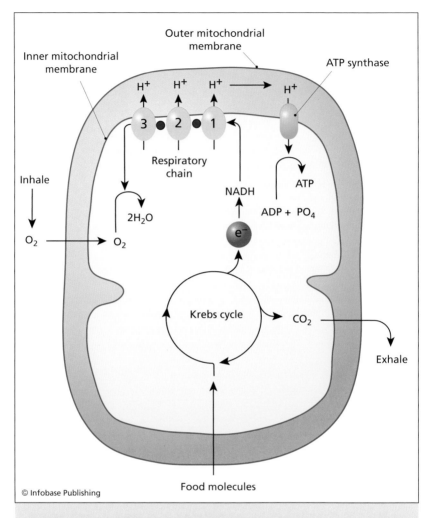

© Infobase Publishing

Production of ATP by mitochondria. Food molecules are processed through the Krebs cycle to produce electrons (e–) that are stored in NADH. The respiratory chain consists of three major components: (1) NADH dehydrogenase, (2) cytochrome b, and (3) cytochrome oxidase. The first component in the chain captures the stored electrons by separating NADH into NAD and H^+ (not shown). The electrons travel through the chain powering a pumping function of each component, resulting in a proton (H^+) concentration gradient across the inner membrane. The electrons are eventually transferred to oxygen (O_2), leading to the production of water. The protons, moving down their concentration gradient, power the synthesis of ATP by the synthase. The only exhaust from this power plant is water, which the cell uses, and CO_2, a gas that is exhaled by the lungs.

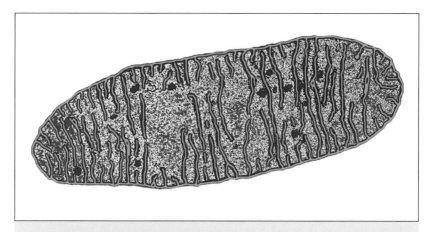

A typical mitochondrion from the pancreas. This image was obtained with a transmission electron microscope. Magnification: 45,000×. *(Dr. Donald Fawcett and Dr. Porter/Visuals Unlimited)*

chain by the iron and copper, as though they were traveling along an electrical wire. All electrical circuits must have a ground; that is, the electrons need someplace to go once they have completed the circuit. In the case of the respiratory chain, the ground is oxygen. After passing through cytochrome oxidase, the last component in the chain, the electrons are picked up by oxygen, which combines with hydrogen ions to form water. As the electrons travel from one end of the chain to the other they energize an ion-pumping function of each protein complex, leading to the movement of hydrogen ions (H^+) across the inner membrane (the same H^+ produced when NADH dehydrogenase releases the electrons by separating NADH into NAD and H^+). The H^+ pass through the ATP synthase and thereby energize the synthesis of ATP from ADP and inorganic phosphate (P_i).

The respiratory chain is a complex system that plays a crucial role in the formation of ATP. A central feature of this system is the use of iron and copper to provide electric power to the three ion-pumping stations that are part of the chain. This system was originated by prokaryotes at least 2 billion years ago, and it provides a highly efficient method for extracting energy from the food one eats. Yet despite its ingenuity, it is not necessarily the best design possible, for there are other metals, such as gold and silver, that are much better electrical conductors than are iron or copper. But one cannot blame the prokaryotes for this; they designed the respiratory chain around iron and copper simply because those metals were much more abundant than gold or silver. The fact that the respiratory chain is iron and copper-based is simply an artifact of Earth's geology. Likewise, human electricians use copper wires, not gold or silver wires, simply because copper is readily available and relatively cheap.

Because gold and silver are nearly 10 times better at conducting electricity than copper or iron, one can expect that a respiratory chain based on gold and silver would be much more efficient than the current one, being able to produce a much greater quantity of ATP in a shorter period of time. This would have the effect of reducing the onset of fatigue, perhaps indefinitely. With gene therapy, the prospect of converting human physiology to a gold- and silver-based respiratory chain is within the realm of possibility. This would require a detailed analysis of the proteins making up the major components of the chain so they may be modified to enhance their binding to gold and silver, rather than copper and iron. With such an analysis at hand, genes could be designed to code for these proteins, after which they would be introduced into human cells.

The respiratory chain is not the only major system that may someday be modified by gene therapy. As mentioned, the ground for the electrons passing through the respiratory chain is oxygen, a major gas in Earth's atmosphere that all animals depend on. The oxygen is picked up in our lungs by hemoglobin, another iron-binding protein complex. All vertebrates use hemoglobin, but many invertebrates, such as crabs and lobsters, prefer a copper-binding protein called hemocyanin. Hemocyanin has an advantage over hemoglobin that explorers and future astronauts may find compelling:

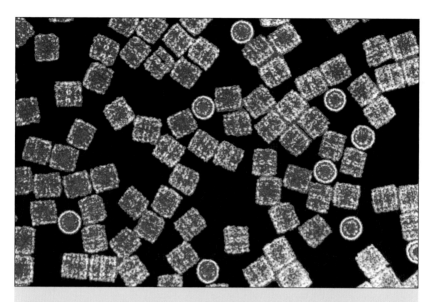

Hemocyanin. Colored transmission electron micrograph (TEM) of molecules of hemocyanin, a respiratory protein and pigment found in mollusks and arthropods. Like hemoglobin in mammals, hemocyanin is an oxygen-carrying molecule. Each molecule is barrel-shaped appearing rounded end-on but oblong with transverse striations when seen from the side. Here, the hemocyanin molecules are from a marine whelk *Burnupena cincta*. They are a copper-containing protein that occurs in solution in mollusk hemolymph "blood." It is blue when oxygenated, colorless when deoxygenated. Magnification: unknown. *(Dr. Linda Stannard, UCT/Photo Researchers, Inc.)*

It has a higher affinity for oxygen and therefore is well suited for environments that have a low oxygen content, such as high altitudes or the surface of other planets. The substitution of hemocyanin for hemoglobin in humans would be much simpler than renovating the respiratory chain. This is because the protein already exists, and the hemocyanin gene has been isolated from invertebrates. The hemocyanin gene could be inserted into human cells and both the old and new genes designed in such a way that they could be turned on or off at will depending on the need. An astronaut visiting an oxygen-depleted world could turn off the hemoglobin gene, turn on the hemocyanin gene, and then switch back once the mission was completed.

Swapping metal ions, in blood pigments or the respiratory chain, would have profound effects on our physiology. Indeed, these simple differences in the metallic content of crucial proteins, based on local geology, are likely be the source of major differences between the people of Earth and creatures (if any) that evolved on other planets. Aside from functional differences, these changes would also affect an individual's appearance. Human skin tone (aside from melanin coloring) is determined by the iron in our blood and in the respiratory chain. Substitute hemocyanin for hemoglobin and the blood becomes pale blue (the color of crab blood). Substitute gold and silver in the respiratory system for copper and iron, and our skin tone would shift to a golden or silver hue.

Some scientists have speculated about the possibility of using gene therapy to improve intelligence, reverse the aging process, and dampen aggressive behavior. However, these would be extremely difficult tasks to accomplish. The main problem is that intelligence, aging, and behavior are controlled by many genes, none of which have so far been identified. But even if they were, it is difficult enough to manage single-gene therapy, let alone trying to insert a dozen or more genes in their proper places and have them all function according to plan. Routine single-gene therapy is still five to 10 years into the future, and multi-gene therapy to influence complex physiological processes will not even be approachable for many years beyond that.

Cosmetic Gene Therapy

Skin color, eye color, hair color, baldness, height, and weight are all physical characteristics that could be modified with gene therapy. Giant fish have already been produced by introducing extra copies of the growth hormone (GH) gene that stimulates bone and muscle growth. Parents who want their children to be really big could have them injected with a GH-vector soon after birth or any time before they enter puberty in order to maximize their size. They could also elect to have their children injected with a melanin-stimulating or melanin-inhibiting vector depending on whether they want their children's skin to be dark or light. Hair and eye color could be controlled just as easily by substituting the child's natural color genes with others of their choice.

Of course, adults will also want to make similar changes to themselves. Baldness is a condition that many men and a few women will choose to treat with gene therapy. There would be no contest between this approach and hair implants or the use of a wig. Hair dyeing is another cosmetic alteration that is commonly performed by adults. Gene therapy could permanently restore the hair's natural color or make it a different color altogether.

None of the cosmetic applications of gene therapy are currently available owing to the danger of the procedure. The cosmetics industry, however, will bring these applications to market as soon as a safe delivery system is available. Whether people will subject themselves or be allowed to subject their children to physiological or cosmetic gene therapy will be discussed in the next chapter.

Bizarre Gene Therapy

How bizarre could gene therapy become? Could ancient myths of wizards and witches casting spells on people to turn them into frogs or monsters become a reality? Does gene therapy have such power?

If one can use gene therapy to treat baldness, one can use it to grow hair over an entire body. Add in a gene to stimulate the growth of canine teeth, and a human could easily be converted into something right out of *Beauty and the Beast*. If one can use gene therapy to darken or lighten the skin, one could also use it to make someone's skin bright red or green or any color for which a gene has been isolated. Scientists have already produced green-glowing

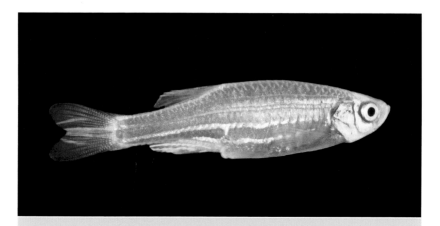

Genetically engineered zebrafish danio *(Brachydanio rerio)* This individual carries DNA from a jellyfish that causes the fish to appear bright orange under normal lights and to fluoresce under ultraviolet (UV) light. *(Edward Kinsman/Photo Researchers, Inc.)*

monkeys and transgenic zebrafish that are bright orange instead of their natural gray-and-white stripes.

Gene therapy can also be used to modify body weight, but in the wrong hands it could be used to make people really fat or extremely thin. Opening our genome to the whole world and then providing that world with a technology for accessing and altering the information contained therein is a very risky business. No one knows how it will play out. The danger to society could be unleashed intentionally or accidentally. For instance, a research lab working on a vector to grow hair could suffer a breach in its containment facility, leading to widespread infection of a local community with possibly devastating consequences. Or bioterrorists might devise a vector carrying a gene for a neurotoxin that could render people unconscious within a few hours. Viewed in this way, the future of gene therapy could hold perils that far exceed the threat of conventional germ warfare.

7

Ethical Issues

The ethical problems associated with gene therapy are the same as those pertaining to any biomedical research that uses humans as experimental subjects. The development of a code of ethics governing these situations can be traced back to the Nuremberg Trials, which convened immediately after World War II to prosecute Nazi war criminals. In the course of those trials, evidence was presented regarding the use of concentration camp prisoners as research subjects. As a consequence, the Nuremberg code of ethics was formalized, and was later expanded on by the Belmont Report, produced in the United States, to address a severe breach in research ethics that surfaced in Tuskegee, Alabama, in 1972.

THE BELMONT REPORT

The U.S. Public Health Service conducted a clinical study involving 600 low-income African-American males in a study dealing with the progression of syphilis in Tuskegee, Alabama. These patients, 400 of whom were infected with syphilis, were monitored for 40 years. The infected individuals were never told they had syphilis but instead told that their medical problems were due to "bad blood." In 1947, penicillin became widely available and was known throughout the medical world as an effective treatment for syphilis, yet the participants in the Tuskegee study were never told there was an antibiotic available that could cure them. The study was terminated in 1972 after its existence was leaked by the press, and it became a political embarrassment. By the time the study was terminated, 28 of the men had died of syphilis, 100 others were dead from related complications, 40 of the participants' wives had been infected, and 19 children had contracted the disease at birth. Public revulsion over the details of this study was instrumental in forcing the government to introduce new policies and laws regarding the use of human subjects in medical research.

On July 12, 1975, the National Research Act was signed into law, thereby creating a national commission to protect human research subjects. This commission was charged with the task of identifying basic ethical principles that should govern the conduct of any research involving human subjects. In February 1976, the commission produced the Belmont Report, so named because the report was finalized at the Smithsonian Institution's Belmont Conference Center. The report began by defining three basic ethical principles that should be applied to research involving human subjects: respect for persons, beneficence, and justice.

Respect for Persons

Respect for persons demands that subjects enter into research voluntarily and with adequate information. This assumes the individuals are autonomous agents—that is, they are competent to make up their own minds. However, there are many instances where potential research subjects are not really autonomous: prisoners, patients in a mental institution, children, the elderly, and the infirm. All of these people require special protection to ensure they are not being coerced or fooled into volunteering as research subjects. The subjects in the Tuskegee study were all poor, uneducated farmworkers who were especially vulnerable to coercion.

Beneficence

Beneficence is generally regarded as acts of kindness or charity, but the report insisted that in the case of research subjects it be made an obligation. In this sense, it is the natural extension of the Hippocratic oath that all physicians are expected to adhere to: *I will give no deadly medicine to anyone if asked, nor suggest any such counsel.* In other words, physicians should do no harm and those involved in biomedical research should never injure one person to benefit another.

Justice

Justice is an extension of beneficence. Researchers must never enlist subjects in an experiment if those subjects do not stand to reap any benefits. The exploitation of prisoners in Nazi concentration camps benefited the Nazis but certainly not the people they experimented on. A second example cited by the Belmont Report was the Tuskegee study. Aside from committing a gross deviation from the most basic of ethical standards, the designers of the Tuskegee study enlisted only black people even though they are not the only racial group to suffer from this disease. The principle of justice was clearly not applied to these subjects.

Guided by these three ethical principles, the Belmont Report introduced the following requirements that all human research trials must adhere to: informed consent, risk/benefit assessment, and fair selection of research subjects.

Informed Consent

All participants must provide informed consent, in writing. Moreover, steps must be taken to ensure the consent is, in fact, informed. This might involve an independent assessment of the individual's ability to understand the language on the consent form and any instructions or explanations the investigators have given. Since the Gelsinger trial, this process was amended to include a patient advocate, present at any meeting between the physicians and the prospective volunteers. This approach has the added advantage of ensuring that scientists do not give prospective subjects misleading or inaccurate information or try to coerce them in any way.

Risk/Benefit Assessment

There is no point in having an ethical standard based on doing no harm if there is no formalized method available for assessing the risk to a patient. It is the risk that is paramount in a patient's mind. No matter how grand the possible benefits, few would volunteer if they thought they would die as a consequence. The only exception to this might be terminally ill patients who volunteer for a clinical trial, even though they know they are not likely to survive it. In general, risks should be reduced to those necessary to achieve the research objective. Risk assessment must be monitored by independent committees based on information supplied by the investigators. If there is significant risk, review committees are expected to demand a justification for it.

Selection of Subjects

The selection process must be fair. Low-risk, potentially beneficial research should not be offered to one segment of our society, while high-risk research is conducted on prisoners, low-income groups, or anyone in a disadvantaged social position.

Conclusions

The Belmont Report introduced, for the first time, the principle of informed consent. Backing this up is the recommendation for independent review committees that ensure the ethical guidelines are being followed. In the United States, the Food and Drug Administration (FDA) and the National Institutes of Health (NIH) are responsible for enforcing the guidelines laid out by the Belmont Report. There are, in addition, local review committees (called institutional review boards) that must approve any experimentation using human subjects. The Belmont Report was inspired by the public's anger over the Tuskegee study. It was fitting that on May 16, 1997, the surviving members of the Tuskegee study were invited to the White House where President Bill Clinton issued a formal apology and reaffirmed the nation's commitment to rigorous ethical standards in biomedical research. No one would have believed at that time that further trouble was just around the corner.

BIOMEDICAL RESEARCH

The investigation into the Gelsinger trial concluded just three years after President Clinton's apology to the Tuskegee patients. While the abuses in this later trial are not as serious, they are of a similar kind. The investigation charged the researchers with essentially four violations: 1) failure to adhere to stopping rules; 2) failure to adhere to the principle of informed consent; 3) failure to keep adequate records; and 4) changing the protocol without approval. Of these charges, the first and second are clear violations of even the most basic of ethical standards.

The principle of informed consent is central to society's acceptance of the use of humans as experimental subjects for biomedical research. This type of research is known as clinical trials. There is, however, a tendency for some people in both the science community and the general public to think of clinical trials as routine medical procedures. They are not. Clinical trials are experiments, and while scientists may claim confidence in the outcome, they really do not know how things will work out; that is after all the basic nature of the research process. To give the public or the research subjects any other impression is unethical behavior. That being the case, there can be no excuse for any deviation from the principle of informed consent. Any patient will give consent to an experimental therapy if he or she expects to be cured or at least be no worse off. All the participants in the Gelsinger trial believed that the worst side effects of the treatment would be a cold or a flu. The researchers did not tell them about the prior death of a monkey treated with a similar protocol, nor did they make it clear to the prospective patients that they might suffer excessive fever or organ damage. Even when some of the patients in the study began to develop these symptoms, the researchers did not tell the other members of the study, thus failing again to adhere to the basic intent of informed consent.

Failure to adhere to the stopping rules is, in a sense, another failure of informed consent; had the investigators stopped one co-hort, it would have been a signal to the other cohorts and to the NIH that something was wrong. Failure to abide by their own protocol suggests the possibility that the researchers included the safeguards only to get federal approval for the study, not to protect the health and interests of their human subjects.

An important lesson to be learned from the Gelsinger trial is that scientists involved in clinical trials cannot be trusted to act ethically as long as they have a financial stake in the outcome. Wilson's company funded much of the research leading up to the trial and, by taking out a patent on the vector design, stood to earn a great deal of money if the procedure worked. This question of the investigator's financial stake in the outcome applies to a great many procedures in biomedical research, including stem cell research, animal cloning, and even clinical trials testing artificial hearts. In practice, a clear separation between the investigators and the possibility of personal financial gain will be almost impossible to guarantee, simply because so many clinical trials are dependent on biotech or pharmaceutical companies for funding. Consequently, the general public will have to put their faith in federal agencies, such as FDA and NIH, to develop enforceable guidelines for gene therapy trials—and indeed for all medical research trials—so everyone involved will have a clear idea of what is going on, who stands to profit by it, and what the risks are.

PHYSIOLOGICAL ENHANCEMENT

It is almost certain that future gene therapies will not be restricted to curing diseases but will also be used to enhance human physiology. Procedures to alter our basic physiology could come from the medical community or from privately owned pharmaceutical and biotech companies. Although the medical profession is primarily concerned with curing diseases, it also provides a great range of surgical procedures that are essentially cosmetic in nature. Patients who want to change the shape of their noses (rhinoplasty) or faces are not confronted with an ethical dilemma. In such cases, the only problem to work out is the question of who pays the bill. Medical insurance companies generally refuse to pay for elective or cosmetic surgery, so payment is the patient's responsibility.

However, physiological enhancement has the potential for serious ethical problems depending on the details of the procedure and whether it is to be done on a consenting adult or on a child. Rhinoplasty is usually performed on adults, and, while the operation changes their appearance, it does not change their genotype. That is, whatever changes are made, they cannot be passed on to successive generations. This may not be the case with a gene therapy trial to alter the respiratory chain or to introduce extra copies of the growth hormone (GH) gene. Even with refined vectors, there is always the possibility the change will affect the gonads, thus altering the individual's germ line. If that happens, the children of those gene therapy subjects stand a chance of inheriting an altered physiology.

The practice of altering human physiology, particularly if it involves the germ line, introduces serious ethical and moral problems, because it presupposes an understanding of nature that society does not possess and is not likely to possess in the foreseeable future. By conducting such experiments, humans remove their evolution from the guidance of natural selection and place it squarely in the hands of a few scientists and technicians who think they know what is best for the future development of our species. Local prejudices and shortsightedness are almost certain to prevail, with the final product being a relatively homogeneous human population, ill-equipped to deal with the realities of the natural world. This situation is equivalent to the genetic bottlenecks that happen occasionally in the natural world. One example is the cheetah, an animal that experienced a near-extinction episode about 100,000 years ago, leaving only a few individuals to reestablish the population. All cheetahs alive today are very closely related; this could be a fatal problem if an unusually virulent bacterial or viral strain ever infects these animals. Human populations have been hit with many such epidemics down through the ages, but it was our genetic diversity that provided the crucial immunity for large numbers of individuals. Tinkering with our genetic heritage, at our current stage of development, might improve our lot, but it could also drive us to the brink of extinction.

COSMETIC APPLICATIONS

The caveats associated with the use of gene therapy for cosmetic purposes are to ensure that it is being done on consenting adults and that the vector will not infect the germ line. But there is a tendency already afoot among some parents who want to fiddle with the appearance of their children. Today, this impulse plays out with the use of GH injections (not gene therapy) to influence the child's size. Gene therapy simply places more options on the table, such as skin and eye color, among others mentioned previously. Children cannot give informed consent; so within the context of the Belmont Report, it is unethical to subject them to these procedures.

Cosmetic applications require careful thought on the part of the medical community or the companies that are offering the treatments. How far should a prospective patient be allowed to go with cosmetic gene therapy? Should consenting adults be allowed to turn their skin bright red or blue if they want to? A current corollary to this problem is the availability of sex-change operations. Is the medical profession adopting an ethical stance by offering such operations or are they simply catering to the delusions of people who may be better served by a psychiatrist?

The search for a cosmetic fix is usually framed in the context of personal freedom, and as long as the treatment is confined to a single individual there is no harm in it. But the use of gene therapy places the question on a different level, simply because of the possible risk of germ line damage or alteration. Ethicists tend to view the germ line as something that belongs to everyone, to the human species, and not to any one individual. Thus, each individual has a responsibility to protect that legacy. This is a concern that society needs to come to grips with now, before the full force of gene therapy becomes a reality.

8

Legal Issues

Gene therapy originated in the United States, primarily through the tireless efforts of Michael Blaese, French Anderson, and their colleagues at the National Institutes of Health (NIH) in Bethesda, Maryland (the location of the DeSilva trial). Thus it was that governmental agencies in the United States were the first to deal with the legal issues associated with gene therapy, and the manner by which they resolved these issues will be the focus of this chapter.

Legislation and regulation of gene therapy is complex and multilayered, involving several U.S. governmental agencies and, in some cases, the courts. It is the nature of the procedure itself that has brought this about. Gene therapy involves a viral vector that is administered to a patient as though it were a drug and so the ultimate regulation of the procedure falls to the Food and Drug Administration (FDA). Other agencies are involved in regulating this procedure by virtue of the fact that they provide financial support for the basic research and the clinical trial. Most gene therapy trials are funded by the NIH, which has special offices and committees that monitor the progress of all such trials to ensure they are conducted according to FDA regulations. In addition, patients involved in gene therapy trials or their families may resort to civil or criminal lawsuits in the event that something goes wrong, especially if it appears to be the fault of the treatment or errors on the part of the investigators. The Gelsinger legal trial will be described later in the chapter as an example of such a lawsuit.

REGULATORY AGENCIES

Although there are many regulatory agencies involved in the control of gene therapy, all of them are under the direction of the FDA or the NIH.

Food and Drug Administration

The FDA is an agency within the Department of Health and Human Services and consists of eight centers and offices that deal with all aspects of food, drug, and radiological safety. The agency currently has a staff of more than 9,000 with a network of 167 field offices. The administration's mission is to promote and protect public health by getting safe and effective products to market as quickly as possible and to continue monitoring product safety after they are in use. The FDA was formed in 1906 when Congress passed the Food and Drugs Act of 1906. The scope of the agency was expanded in 1938 with the passage of the Federal Food, Drug, and Cosmetic Act, giving it the power to ask the courts to issue injunctions or prosecute those who deliberately violate the agency's regulations.

In 1984, the FDA established the Center for Biologics Evaluation and Research (CBER), which has the responsibility of regulating gene therapy. In 1991, CBER issued a document that stipulated the precautions that must be taken in the manufacturing and testing of gene therapy products, thus broadening its scope to include all aspects of gene therapy, from product manufacturing to application

GENE THERAPY REGULATORY AGENCIES AND COMMITTEES IN THE UNITED STATES

NAME	ABBREVIATION
Food and Drug Administration	FDA
Center for Biologics Evaluation and Research (FDA)	CBER
National Institutes of Health	NIH
Office of Biotechnology Activities (NIH)	OBA
Recombinant DNA Advisory Committee (NIH)	RAC
Office of Human Subjects Research (NIH)	OHSR

in clinical trials. As defined by CBER, biologics, unlike the usual kind of drug, are derived from humans, animals, or microorganisms. Most biologics are complex mixtures that are not easily identified or characterized, and many of them are manufactured using biotechnology. In justifying its intent to regulate gene therapy, the FDA and CBER have made it clear that DNA or viral vectors that are administered to gene therapy patients are products that the agency has a mandate to regulate. All gene therapy clinical trials require a license from the FDA, which monitors the progress of all trials through CBER. Investigators must submit regular reports to CBER, and, in some cases, the center will conduct on-site inspections to ensure the trial is following the required guidelines. Both the FDA and the NIH monitor NIH-funded gene therapy trials. The NIH monitoring effort is the responsibility of the Office of Biotechnology Activities, to which the Recombinant DNA Advisory Committee (RAC) belongs, and the Office of Human Subjects Research. If officials at NIH discover a breach in regulations, they are required by law to report it to the FDA, which has the ultimate power to terminate the trial and to order an investigation.

An FDA guidance document has detailed the agency's legal basis for its regulation of gene therapy. The document explains that while the agency was created before the advent of gene therapies, its scope is sufficiently broad to encompass new and unexpected products that require testing and verification prior to marketing. The document defined gene therapy as a medical procedure based on genetic modification of living cells, where the genetic manipulation is intended to treat disease or injuries in humans. According to the document, the products containing the genetic material, either DNA or a viral vector that is intended for gene therapy, are regulated as biological products (biologics) or as drugs. Consequently, gene therapy products require the premarket submission and approval of an application before they may be used in a clinical setting.

The investigator must also submit an investigational new drug application (IND) to the FDA demonstrating that the available preclinical (e.g., animal or laboratory) data justify testing the product on human subjects to see if it is safe and effective. The IND rules also require that the researcher has obtained approval from an institutional review board (IRB). Since the death of Jesse Gelsinger in 1999, FDA and NIH have announced new initiatives to protect participants in gene therapy trials. FDA has suspended gene therapy trials at institutions the agency has found in violation of its requirements. FDA is currently monitoring more than 900 gene therapy trials but has not as yet approved for sale any human gene therapy products.

National Institutes of Health

NIH began as a one-room laboratory of hygiene in 1887 with an annual budget of $300. Since then, it has grown into one of the finest medical research centers in the world with a staff of more than 18,000 employees and an annual budget that exceeded $30 billion in 2009. The mission of NIH is the pursuit of fundamental knowledge of living systems and the application of that knowledge to the treatment of human diseases and disabilities. To that end, more than 325,000 scientists, stationed at NIH laboratories and research centers throughout the country, are funded by NIH. In 2009, 52,000 grants were awarded to researchers at more than 3,000 universities and research institutions. The quality of NIH–funded research is of the highest caliber, with 106 of the grantees having been awarded the Nobel Prize.

In 1974, NIH established the Office of Biotechnology Activities (OBA), which formed the Recombinant DNA Advisory Committee (known as the RAC). This committee was given the responsibility of monitoring and regulating the newly discovered laboratory technique by which the DNA from different organisms could be recombined (termed *recombinant DNA*) to form new and potentially hazardous hybrid molecules and organisms. Initially, the RAC focused on safety concerns relating to the inadvertent release of recombinant DNA into the environment. In 1976, the RAC issued new regulations requiring institutions involved in recombinant DNA research to establish an institutional biohazard committee for on-site regulation of such research.

In 1980, the OBA shifted its attention to the use of recombinant DNA in a newly devised procedure now known as gene therapy. In 1984, the RAC formed the Human Gene Therapy Working Group, consisting of scientists, clinicians, lawyers, ethicists, policy experts, and public representatives. The working group recommended that the RAC broaden its scope to include a review of gene therapy protocols and provided a list of questions and conditions that gene therapists must address in submissions to the RAC. All gene therapy protocols that are funded by NIH or conducted at NIH–funded institutions must be submitted to the RAC for approval. Implementation of a trial protocol, however, cannot proceed without the prior approval of the FDA. Thus, both organizations assume the responsibility of monitoring NIH–funded trials. Gene therapy trials that are not funded by NIH (e.g., trials that are funded by biotech or pharmaceutical companies) require only the approval of the FDA, which takes full responsibility for subsequent monitoring and regulation. The great advantage of NIH–funded gene therapy research from the point of view of the public's safety and concern is that the review process and the monitoring are made public. Indeed, since the death of Jesse Gelsinger, NIH regulations have been modified to include patient advocates and the posting of information on the Internet detailing protocols, progress, and outcomes of NIH–funded clinical trials.

The NIH is also interested in possible future applications of gene therapy and has sponsored a gene therapy policy conference to discuss the use of this procedure for cosmetic enhancement, such as treatments for baldness. While favoring some cosmetic applications, RAC has made it clear that it will not accept proposals for germ line gene transfer experiments. The role of the RAC has evolved over the years from a regulatory body to an agency that provides a much-needed public forum that deals with the legal and ethical issues raised by gene therapy.

THE GELSINGER LEGAL TRIAL

Jesse Gelsinger's death marked a crucial turning point in the regulation of gene therapy trials and in the public's attitude toward clinical trials in general. Initially, Jesse's father, Paul Gelsinger, trusted the medical staff involved in the trial that took his son's life, but as the FDA investigation progressed it became clear to him that he had been naive to have been as trusting as he was. Consequently, in 2000, Paul Gelsinger and his brother John launched a civil lawsuit in which the defendants were the trustees of the University of Pennsylvania, Dr. James Wilson, and the company he cofounded, Genovo, Inc., and the attending physicians, Dr. Steven Raper and Dr. Mark Batshaw. Arthur Caplan, a bioethicist at the University of Pennsylvania, was also included for advice he gave to the other defendants. The lawsuit consisted of the following eight counts, including wrongful death, survival action, strict products liability, intentional assault and battery, intentional and negligent infliction of emotional distress, common law fraud, punitive damages, and fraud on the FDA:

> *Count I—Wrongful Death.* The plaintiffs in the case, Paul and John Gelsinger, charged that "as a result of the careless, negligent and reckless conduct of the defendants herein, Jesse Gelsinger was caused to suffer excruciating and agonizing pain and discomfort and ultimately died as a result of defendants' conduct." The count further charges that the defendants failed to evaluate Jesse Gelsinger properly for admission into the trial and that, once admitted, failed to care for his condition under all of the circumstances and by so doing failed to follow and abide by guidelines set forth by the FDA and NIH.
>
> *Count II—Survival Action.* In causing Jesse Gelsinger's death, the defendants wrongfully deprived him of earnings and the right to earn a living. Consequently, the plaintiffs, acting on behalf of the estate of Jesse Gelsinger, are entitled to recover an amount equal to the gross amount that Jesse would have earned from the date of his death to the end of his normal life expectancy.
>
> *Count III—Strict Products Liability.* James Wilson and Genovo, Inc., manufactured and supplied the AD virus that ultimately caused the death of Jesse Gelsinger. The Institute of Human Gene Therapy (IHGT), as part of the University of Pennsylvania, is equally liable for supplying the same virus as part of the gene therapy trial. The defendants were further charged with designing, manufacturing, and selling a product that was poorly tested, defective, and dangerous. Moreover, the AD virus was sold without proper warnings on the product, and without warning the clinical subjects of the dangers inherent in using the product.

Count IV—Intentional Assault and Battery, Lack of Informed Consent. The defendants failed to warn Jesse Gelsinger of all the risks involved in the therapy without which he could not be expected to have given informed consent. The lack of informed consent involved several points that included, among others, understating the expected toxic effects of the virus and failing to describe the adverse effects experienced by previous patients in the trial and the death of a monkey who received the virus in preclinical trials. The defendants also failed to disclose the financial interest that Dr. Wilson and the university had in relation to the study.

Count V—Intentional and Negligent Infliction of Emotional Distress. Paul Gelsinger's agreement to allow his son to take part in the study was based on the misleading information he was given by the defendants. As a consequence, he has suffered severe emotional distress for which he deserves compensation.

Count VI—Common Law Fraud / Intentional Misrepresentation. The defendants committed fraud by intentionally misrepresenting the risks of the therapy and, in particular, the toxic side effects associated with the injection of the AD virus.

Count VII—Punitive Damages. The plaintiffs maintained that the behavior of the defendants toward Jesse Gelsinger was "intentional, wanton, willful and outrageous. Defendants were grossly negligent, and acted with reckless disregard of and with deliberate, callous and reckless indifference to the rights, interests, welfare and safety of plaintiff's decedent."

Count VIII—Fraud on the FDA. Defendants Batshaw, Raper, Wilson, IHGT, and Genovo "intentionally and falsely made numerous fraudulent misrepresentations to the FDA concerning the protocol of the OTC gene transfer experiment." It was also charged that the defendants altered the FDA approved consent form, deleting any reference to monkeys that became ill and died after receiving a similar AD vector in preclinical trials. Moreover, they defrauded the FDA by failing to report adverse and unexpected reactions associated with the administration of the vector.

Although committed to a jury trial in 2000, the University of Pennsylvania decided to settle out of court by paying the plaintiffs several million dollars in compensation. Paul Gelsinger has vowed to use the money to help improve patient safety in all clinical trials. Dr. Wilson resigned his position as director of IHGT in 2002, and the FDA has barred him from ever conducting further research on humans. Despite his resignation from IHGT, Dr. Wilson retains his faculty position and tenure at the University of Pennsylvania. Alan Milstein, the Gelsinger family's lawyer, has stated that the resignation is an inadequate consequence for Wilson's misdeeds that led to the death of Jesse Gelsinger. For its part, the university has never publicly apologized to the Gelsinger family.

On February 9, 2005, the Department of Justice announced a civil settlement in its five-year investigation into the death of Jesse Gelsinger. The Justice Department asked Paul Gelsinger if he could support the proposed settlement. In a statement published on the Citizens for Responsible Care and Research (CIRCARE) Web site, Paul Gelsinger said that he would support it if he received the following from the responsible parties:

1. A public admission that their violations of the protocol and lack of adherence to the stopping rules directly resulted in Jesse's death.
2. A public apology by all parties for causing Jesse's death and for their deception in the following months.

3. Archiving all the documents related to the experiment so researchers and the media can try to learn what really happened.

We received none of what we asked for and therefore do not support this settlement. There will be no further legal action by the Justice Department in this matter, and the public should be dismayed that the responsible parties were let off so easily. In my conversations with the Justice Department it was evident that Justice does not have statutory authority to go after researchers for wrongful death or manslaughter charges. They are only able to pursue charges related to fraud. Congress needs to work on legislation that will give our national law enforcement agencies the authority they need to curb the type of behavior demonstrated by these researchers and their institutions.

CIRCARE, of which I am vice president, has been dedicated to accountability in research and the passage of legislation that would make it safer for the public in its willingness to participate in clinical research. That effort has long been frustrated by the lobbying efforts of pharmaceutical and biotech companies, and even academia.

The University of Pennsylvania, recognized as America's first university, was founded by the illustrious Benjamin Franklin in 1749 as an institution dedicated to educating young people for the betterment of all society. Nine signers of the Declaration of Independence and 11 signers of the Constitution were associated with the university. The country's first medical school was established there in 1874 and, since 1923, 15 Penn scholars have been awarded Nobel Prizes. For many years, this university has served as a model for research colleges and universities throughout the world.

But this grand institution, by its refusal to offer a simple apology for what happened to Jesse Gelsinger, has increased the public perception that academics, eager to profit from the pharmaceutical industry, have let their greed and arrogance blind them to their original mission, and now stands as a disgrace to the memory of its founder.

As of 2009, the situation has not changed: The Gelsinger family has not been offered an apology and according to Paul Gelsinger and CIRCARE cofounder, Adil Shamoo, patients who enroll in clinical trials are no safer now than they were nine years ago; "they are still at serious risk of exploitation and harm." Part of the problem is the sheer number of trials that need to be monitored. According to CIRCARE, the FDA has only 200 investigators to manage more than 300,000 clinical research sites. It is no wonder that just 1 percent of these sites are ever inspected.

INTERNATIONAL REGULATION

The United Kingdom (U.K.) and the European Union (EU) have formed gene therapy regulatory agencies that are very similar in organization to those established in the United States. Discussions began in 1991 and 1992 and led to the formation of the Gene Therapy Advisory Committee (GTAC) in the U.K. and the European Agency for the Evaluation of Medicinal Products (EMEA) in the EU.

GTAC was established by the U.K. Department of Health in 1993. This committee reviews gene therapy proposals and makes recommendations to the Department of Health as to their acceptability. Their decisions are based on scientific merit and potential benefits and risks. The committee also provides advice to U.K. health ministers on developments in gene therapy. The primary concern of GTAC is whether the gene therapy proposal meets accepted ethical criteria for research on human subjects as laid out by the Belmont Report and the Nuremberg Code. GTAC approval must be obtained before somatic cell gene therapy is conducted on human subjects. In accord with NIH regulations, GTAC will not allow gene therapy trials involving the germ line. This committee takes the view that gene therapy is not really therapy at all but a research procedure, and therefore all such trials must take place under strict rules established by GTAC. In contrast to FDA and NIH regulations, GTAC believes that gene therapy should be limited to life-threatening diseases or disorders. The European regulatory agency, EMEA, is in full accord with GTAC policies.

9

Clinical Trials

Although gene therapy has suffered some major setbacks over the years one would never know it by looking at the number and range of clinical trials that are currently under way. In 2009, there were more than 1,000 gene therapy trials in progress in the United States and Europe. Most of these trials are focused on cancer, but there is an impressive variety of trials attempting to treat immunological disorders, Alzheimer's disease, cardiovascular disease, and cystic fibrosis, to name but a few. The DeSilva trial remains the most successful, but that is likely to change in the very near future.

CANCER

Although many cancers are being treated with gene therapy in clinical trials, very promising results have been obtained with treatments for melanoma and prostate cancer.

Melanoma

Scientists at the National Cancer Institute (NCI) have recently discovered a way to increase the cancer-fighting capabilities of T lymphocytes. Clinical trials involving an immunotherapy known as adoptive cell transfer successfully treated metastatic melanoma in some patients. In those trials, tumor-infiltrating T lymphocytes (TILs) were harvested from the patient's tumors, grown in tissue culture in order to increase their numbers, and then injected back into the patient. These T cells, by virtue of the fact that they had already encountered the tumor, were self-programmed to target an antigen called MART-1, which is found on the surface of all melanoma cells. Thus, expanding their population in culture and then injecting them back into the patient greatly increases their ability to destroy the cancer cells.

Unfortunately, TILs cannot be isolated from most patients suffering from melanoma. In order to make this a practical strategy, scientists at NCI, led by Stephen Rosenberg, converted ordinary T cells into TILs. This was accomplished by inserting the gene for the MART-1 receptor into T cells isolated from a patient using gene therapy. These cells were then grown in culture to increase their numbers before injecting them back into the patient. Thus, the patient's T cells were genetically engineered to recognize and attack cancer cells. The MART-1 receptor, known as a tumor cell receptor (TCR), makes it possible for the T cell to bind to, and destroy, the cancer cell. This procedure was tested on 17 patients, several of whom experienced cancer regression (i.e., the tumors were destroyed). One month after treatment, 14 of the patients still had 9 percent to 56 percent of their genetically engineered T cells. There were no toxic side effects in any of the patients.

These results, published in the journal *Science* in 2006, represent the first time gene therapy has been used to successfully treat a cancer. Dr. Rosenberg's team is now trying to improve the effectiveness of this therapy by developing TCRs that bind more effectively to the cancer cells. They have also isolated TCRs that recognize common cancers other than melanoma.

Prostate Cancer

Researchers from Columbia University in New York City have developed a novel gene therapy technique that uses a virus engineered to replicate only within cancer cells and produce a protein toxic to those cells. The results of their preclinical laboratory studies showed complete eradication of both primary and distant tumors in a mouse model of prostate cancer.

The investigators built their system around a gene called *Mda-7/IL-24,* which codes for the cytokine IL-24. This protein is produced by immune cells and can kill cancer cells when it is secreted at high levels. An adenovirus (AD) was modified not only to carry the gene, but also to multiply only within cancer cells. This was accomplished by linking viral reproduction to the activity of transcription factors found only in cancer cells. When the virus enters a cancer cell it replicates millions of copies of itself and produces IL-24, which kills the cell and releases a flood of virus into the bloodstream to infect and kill other cancer cells.

After in vitro experiments confirmed that viral replication was confined to cancer cells and induced growth inhibition and cell death, the investigators tested their gene therapy system in a xenograft mouse model of therapy-resistant prostate cancer. In this case, the virus completely eradicated not only the primary tumor but also distant tumors. This type of therapy, known as adenovirus-mediated suicide gene therapy, has been tested in a Phase I clinical trial, producing a moderate clinical response in several patients after a 90-day treatment cycle.

CYSTIC FIBROSIS

Cystic fibrosis (CF), described in chapter 2, is a degenerative disease of the lungs that is often fatal. This disease is an ideal candidate for gene therapy for the following reasons:

1. It is a single gene (monogenic) defect.
2. The most severely affected organ is the lung, which is readily accessible for treatment.
3. Heterozygote carriers of the CF gene have about 50 percent sodium chloride transporter (CFTR) function, yet are completely asymptomatic, suggesting a broad window for effective CFTR function. Indeed, studies have shown that only about 5 to 10 percent of normal CFTR function is required to reverse ion transport defects, effectively curing the disease.
4. The disease progresses very slowly, providing time for the therapy to work before the lungs are damaged.

Despite these promising characteristics, progress with CF gene therapy has been much slower than researchers had predicted. Clinical trials have demonstrated that a normal CF gene can be delivered to the respiratory tract, but it is expressed at very low levels and for only about 30 days. Attempts to extend this time period have been frustrated by the natural turnover of the bronchial epithelium, which has a life span of about 120 days. Thus, even with an ideal vector, patients would have to be dosed repeatedly in order to maintain the therapy.

The first human CF gene therapy trial was conducted in New York in 1993, just two years after the success of the DeSilva trial. Four volunteers with CF received an AD vector containing the CFTR gene. This vector was administered to their noses as a nasal spray and one day later to their lungs using a bronchoscope. Although there was evidence for the expression of the normal CFTR gene, the effect lasted for only 10 days, at which time the trial was terminated due to extensive pulmonary inflammation (i.e., the patients developed a severe vector-induced flu). In 1995, a research group in North Carolina conducted a similar trial on 11 volunteers, using a slightly modified AD vector. In this case, only 1 percent of the nasal epithelium showed evidence of being transfected and again the patients all suffered pulmonary inflammation, ruling out the possibility of increasing the vector dose. In 1999, the New York group conducted a new trial using a different strain of AD virus in the hope of reducing the inflammation that had plagued previous trials. The 14 subjects were given the vector as described above, only in this case they received three separate doses three months apart. Although the inflammation was less than in the previous study, the effectiveness of the vector decreased markedly with each dose. This meant that the immune system was sensitized to the presence of the vector with the first dose and effectively eliminated the vector in subsequent doses before they could infect the target cells. This trial, along with all others involving AD vectors, was terminated immediately after the death of Jesse Gelsinger in September 1999.

More recently, researchers at Stanford University and the University of Washington, Seattle, have been testing the adeno-associated virus (AAV) in two different CF clinical trials. Although AAV and AD have similar names, they are not related. AAV does not cause any known human diseases, and for this reason scientists believed it would not cause an inflammation of the lungs. This assumption was confirmed after both groups tested this new vector on a total of 22 subjects. The effectiveness of AAV was then tested on 37 subjects in a randomized, multicenter trial coordinated by the Stanford group. The results of this trial were very encouraging, as there was a marked improvement in respiratory function and a reduction in the inflammatory response. On the other hand, the effectiveness of the vector decreased with each subsequent dose, just as it did with the AD vectors.

Currently, clinical trials are testing viral and liposome vectors that target lung tissue and maintain a high level of expression in the absence of inflammation. Liposome vectors (described in chapter 6) hold great promise because they do not elicit an immune response and thus are not likely to cause an inflammatory response. On the other hand, these vectors have proved to be very inefficient at delivering the vector to the targeted cells. Consequently, although the expression of the normal CFTR was observed, the level was not high enough to affect the clinical symptoms of the disease. Modest results such as these have been obtained in several clinical trials involving more than 90 subjects.

Researchers are working to improve the efficiency of liposome vectors and to enhance the utilization of the normal CFTR gene once it gains access to the cell. Studies have shown that much of the gene remains in the cytoplasm where it is not transcribed. This is thought be the main reason for the low level of expression regardless of which kind of vector is used. To deal with this problem, future trials will use a CFTR gene that is tagged with a nuclear localization sequence (NLS) in order to get more of the gene inside the nucleus. Investigators designing clinical trials using viral vectors are also considering the possibility of placing the subjects on immunosuppressants during the course of treatment to reduce the incidence of inflammation and to increase the likelihood of cells becoming infected with the vector. Although the initial goal was a single gene-correcting therapy that would cure CF for the life of the patient, it now appears that the therapy will need to be repeated several times a year in order to control the symptoms of this disease.

IMMUNOLOGICAL DISORDERS

As described in chapter 2, immune deficiencies appear in essentially two forms. The first is caused by adenosine deaminase (ADA) deficiency, which is what Ashi DeSilva suffered from; the second, known as X-linked severe combined immunodeficiency (SCID-X1), results from a gene mutation that disrupts communication between white blood cells. SCID-X1 has been studied intensively for more than 10 years and was the subject of one of the most successful clinical trials of recent years.

X-Linked Severe Combined Immunodeficiency (SCID-X1)

The gene therapy trial for SCID-X1, conducted by Dr. Alain Fischer and his team at the Necker Hospital in Paris, France, is possibly the most important gene therapy trial to be launched since 1990. This trial, introduced in chapter 6, used a novel combination of gene therapy and stem cell therapy to treat SCID-X1. This form of immunodeficiency is caused by a mutation in a gene coding for the gamma chain (γC) of an interleukin receptor that occurs in the membranes of all lymphocytes. (The gene for γC is referred to as γ_c.) Interleukin receptors are dimeric or trimeric, that is, they consist of two or three polypeptide chains (β and γ or α, β, and γ) that span the cell membrane. The dimeric form is a receptor for IL4, IL7, IL9, and IL21. The trimeric form (known as IL2R) is a receptor for IL2 and IL15. Thus, a mutation in γ_c destroys the cell's ability to receive signals from six interleukins. This not only interferes with the activation and maturation of T cells but it also interferes with the normal development of NK cells and B cells. Consequently, children born with this defect are incapable of mounting an adaptive immune response.

Fischer's team developed a different protocol from that used in the DeSilva trial. Instead of transfecting isolated lymphocytes, they harvested stem cells from each patient's bone marrow. These cells are known as hematopoietic stem cells (HSCs). The HSCs were transfected in cell culture with a normal copy of the γ_c gene, carried by a retrovirus vector, and then reintroduced into the bloodstream of the patient. The advantage of this approach is that the genetically corrected stem cells could reconstitute a healthy population of white blood cells and would continue doing so for the life of the patient. In the case of the DeSilva trial, lymphocytes were transfected and reintroduced into the patient's bloodstream, but once these genetically corrected cells had died they were replaced by defective lymphocytes, since the patient's stem cells had not been corrected. Thus, in the case of DeSilva, genetically corrected lymphocytes had to be reintroduced at regular intervals in order to maintain a functional immune system.

In the Fischer trial, 10 patients were treated, all of whom showed a dramatic improvement in their immune response, characterized by an increase in the number of T, B, and NK cells. The overall profile of the patients' immune systems, with regard to the number and function of the lymphocytes, was shown to be similar to that of age-matched controls. But in January 2003, two of the patients (P4 and P5) were diagnosed with T cell leukemia and, by the end of that year, researchers had determined that the cancerous cells could be traced to the genetically modified stem cells. It was also shown that the retrovirus used in the trial caused the cancers by inserting within or near an oncogene known as *LMO2*.

Immediately after the cancer cases were diagnosed, regulatory agencies in Europe and the United States stopped all gene therapy trials involving retroviral vectors. In March 2003, the Food and Drug Administration (FDA), and equivalent European agencies agreed to lift the ban after carefully considering the following points: First, the majority of the children in the Fischer trial showed major improvements in their overall health and are now able to live normal lives; second, the complication of leukemia has not occurred in any of the more than 250 patients currently enrolled in more than 40 clinical trials involving retroviral vectors; finally, the incidence of adverse effects was deemed to be too low to justify cessation of other retroviral gene transfer studies.

Patients P4 and P5 were treated with chemotherapy, and, while P5 is now doing well, P4 did not respond to the therapy. Despite a second round of chemotherapy, treatment with a monoclonal antibody, and a bone marrow transplant, the child died in 2008. Shortly before the death of P4, two additional patients (P7 and P10) developed leukemia. Both patients were treated for acute lymphoblastic leukemia, and after two cycles both patients, now under supportive care, are in complete remission and doing well.

When the Fischer trial began in 1998, most scientists did not consider the possibility of cancers being induced by the vector. The main concern was to avoid the kind of complications that arose during the Gelsinger trial. It is now clear, however, that insertional mutagenesis, caused by the vector, is a very serious problem that needs to be overcome before gene therapy can become a practical reality. Scientists in the United States and Europe are now identifying all retroviral integration sites (RISs) in the human and mouse genomes (determination of RISs in the mouse genome is important for preclinical research). This search is conducted by transfecting cells in culture and then, using PCR and other methods, mapping out the chromosomal location of the RIS and the exact sequence around the insertion site. This information will make it possible to identify or design vectors that insert in gene-poor regions, far away from any known oncogenes.

NEUROLOGICAL DISORDERS

Diseases in this category, such as Alzheimer's disease (AD), Parkinson's disease, and Huntington's disease (HD), are among the most difficult disorders to study and to treat. These diseases affect the brain, the most complex organ known to science and one that is still poorly understood. Nevertheless, some progress has been made with gene therapies, which either block a mutant protein responsible for the disorder, as is the case for HD, or stimulate the production of molecules that can alleviate the symptoms of the disease, as is being done for AD and Parkinson's disease.

Alzheimer's Disease

In April 2004, a research team at the University of California, San Diego, headed by Dr. Mark Tuszynski, reported some success in a Phase I clinical trial to treat AD. Tuszynski's team began by isolating skin cells from each of eight patients recruited for the study and transfected those cells with a vector carrying a gene coding for nerve growth factor (NGF). In preclinical studies, other researchers have shown that NGF, a protein, appears to help neurons resist the kind of degeneration that is typical of AD. The genetically modified skin cells were injected into the brains of the eight patients.

Since each patient received an injection of his or her own genetically modified cells, immune rejection was not a problem. One year later, the patients' rate of mental decline was reduced by half. By comparison, currently available drug therapies reduce mental decline by only 5 percent.

Tuszynski's team is currently preparing to launch a larger follow-up study to confirm these results. This study not only represents a successful gene therapy trial but is the first time a therapy of any kind has actually prevented cell death in patients suffering from AD. It must be noted, however, that this form of AD therapy is risky. The first two patients received their injections of the modified skin cells under local anesthesia. One of these patients moved during the procedure and subsequently died from a brain hemorrhage. The remaining subjects were injected under a general anesthetic. All of these subjects recovered fully from the operation, but the long-term effects of this procedure on a large number of subjects are yet to be determined.

Huntington's Disease

The neurological damage caused by HD is due to the buildup of the mutant Huntington protein. Researchers have reasoned that even without correcting the gene it could be possible to treat this disease by deactivating the mRNA used by the cell to synthesize the protein. This form of gene therapy is known as RNA interference. Dr. Beverly Davidson at the University of Iowa has reported the results of two preclinical studies in mice that involved a disorder similar to HD, known as spinocerebellar ataxia, which affects the animal's ability to walk.

Davidson's team produced a vector containing a therapeutic DNA molecule with a base sequence complementary to the ataxia mRNA. In vivo hybridization between the mRNA and the therapeutic DNA was expected to block the translation of the mRNA. After injecting the vector into the mice, the researchers found that the production of the defective protein was indeed blocked and the mice seemed to improve. They also tested their procedure on human cells in culture, where they were able to block the production of the Huntington's protein. Davidson is now planning to test this very promising procedure in a Phase I human trial.

Parkinson's Disease

An American team, led by Dr. Michael Kaplitt, has reported success with a small trial involving 12 subjects. Although the usual target in this disease is dopaminergic neurons, this trial was conducted with a viral vector containing the gene for glutamic acid decarboxylase (GAD). This enzyme produces gamma butyric acid (GABA), a neurotransmitter released by neurons to inhibit or dampen the activity of the brain's circuitry. The scientists reasoned that extra copies of GAD would increase the levels of GABA, thereby reducing the intensity of the muscle spasms associated with this neurological disorder. The vector was injected directly into the brain as was done for the Tuszynski AD trial described above. The results showed that the patients' symptoms were improved by up to 65 percent after the first year, with no side effects.

Another trial, led by Dr. Philip Starr at the University of California, San Francisco (UCSF), treated 12 patients with a vector carrying a gene for a NGF. Standard treatments can reduce the tremors but do not prevent the death of the dopamine-producing neurons. The object of this trial was to rescue dying neurons by stimulating neural growth and repair. The vector was delivered to a specific site in the brain following the methods of the Tuszynski trial. One year after the treatment, nine patients experienced a 38 percent improvement with no serious side effects. These results, encouraging though they are, will have to be confirmed on a larger number of patients. The UCSF team is in the process of recruiting 56 subjects who will take part in a more elaborate trial in which some of the subjects will undergo sham surgery (i.e., the brain is injected with a solution that does not contain the vector). These subjects, known as the control group, will be compared to the experimental group for a better estimate of how well the therapy works.

RETINAL DYSTROPHY

Preclinical research has shown that retinal dystrophy in mice and dogs is not always associated with degeneration of the retinal hardware (i.e., the rods and cones) even though the animals suffer from severe visual impairment. This is a crucial finding, since gene therapy would have little effect if the cells themselves were dead or dying. In 2003, researchers at the University of Missouri–Columbia were able to restore the vision in five dogs suffering from retinal dystrophy with *RPE65* gene replacement therapy.

A preliminary clinical trial involving 59 subjects, 21 of whom had normal vision, has confirmed the surprisingly healthy structure of dystrophic retinas. Using high-resolution microscopy, the investigators were able to show that nearly half of the subjects with R91W or Y36H mutations (i.e., mutations affecting *RPE65,* described in chapter 2) had normal retinal structure, including healthy-looking rods, cones, and pigmented epithelium.

In 2007, British researchers at University College London (UCL) began testing *RPE65* gene therapy on patients suffering from retinal dystrophy. The therapy, applied to only one eye of each patient, was performed by inserting the needle of a syringe through the eye and injecting the *RPE65* vector directly into the retina. In 2008, the group, led by Dr. Robin Ali, announced that one of the patients began seeing the outlines of various shapes within a month of being treated and eventually showed a dramatic improvement in his night vision. They tested this by having the patient navigate a constructed simulation of a nighttime scene. Before the operation he was barely able to navigate the scene but after treatment was able to do it quickly and without mistakes.

10

Resource Center

Gene therapy depends on a thorough understanding of cell biology and biotechnology, both of which require a great deal of laboratory equipment and experimental procedures. This chapter provides brief discussions of cell biology and recombinant DNA technology, also known as biotechnology.

CELL BIOLOGY

A cell is a microscopic life-form made from a variety of nature's building blocks. The smallest of these building blocks are subatomic particles known as quarks and leptons that form protons, neutrons, and electrons, which in turn form atoms. Scientists have identified more than 200 atoms, each of which represents a fundamental element of nature. Carbon, oxygen, and nitrogen are common examples. Atoms, in their turn, can associate with each other to form another

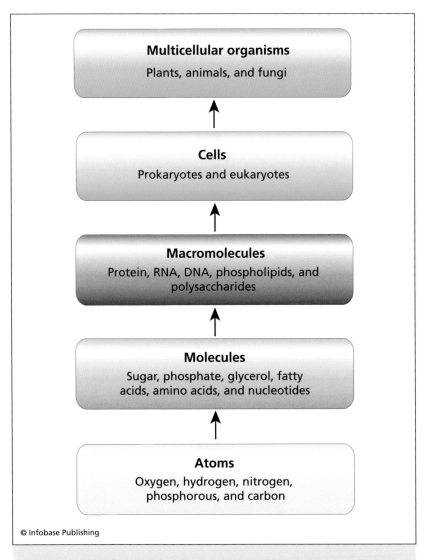

Nature's building blocks. Particles known as quarks and leptons, created in the heat of the big bang, formed the first atoms, which combined to form molecules in the oceans of the young Earth. Heat and electrical storms promoted the formation of macromolecules, providing the building blocks for cells, which in turn went on to form multicellular organisms.

kind of building block known as a molecule. Sugar, for example, is a molecule constructed from carbon, oxygen, and hydrogen, while ordinary table salt is a molecule consisting of sodium and chloride. Molecules can link up with each other to form yet another kind of building block known as a macromolecule. Macromolecules, present in the atmosphere of the young Earth, gave rise to cells, which in turn went on to form multicellular organisms. In forming those organisms, cells became a new kind of building block.

The Origin of Life

Molecules essential for life are thought to have formed spontaneously in the oceans of the primordial Earth about 4 billion years ago. Under the influence of a hot stormy environment, the molecules combined to produce macromolecules, which in turn formed microscopic bubbles that were bounded by a sturdy macromolecular membrane analogous to the skin on a grape. It took about half a billion years for the prebiotic bubbles to evolve into the first cells, known as prokaryotes, and another 1 billion years for those cells to evolve into the eukaryotes. Prokaryotes, also known as bacteria, are small cells (about five micrometers in diameter) that have a relatively simple structure and a genome consisting of about 4,000 genes. Eukaryotes are much larger (about 30 micrometers in diameter), with a complex internal structure and a very large genome, often exceeding 20,000 genes. These genes are kept in a special organelle called the nucleus (eukaryote means "true nucleus"). Prokaryotes are all single-cell organisms, although some can form short chains or temporary fruiting bodies. Eukaryotes, on the other hand, gave rise to all of the multicellular plants and animals that now inhabit the Earth.

A Typical Eukaryote

Eukaryotes assume a variety of shapes that are variations on the simple spheres from which they originated. Viewed from the side, they often have a galactic profile, with a central bulge (the nucleus)

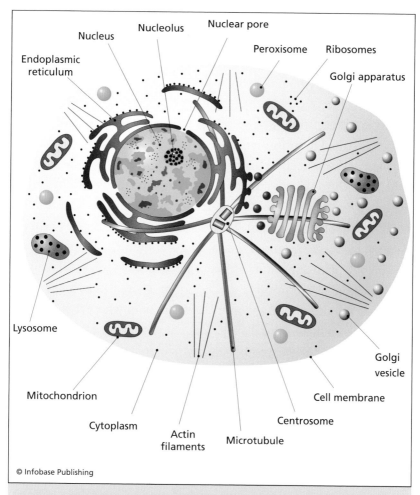

Nucleus
Nucleolus
Nuclear pore
Peroxisome
Ribosomes
Endoplasmic reticulum
Golgi apparatus
Lysosome
Mitochondrion
Cytoplasm
Actin filaments
Microtubule
Centrosome
Cell membrane
Golgi vesicle

© Infobase Publishing

The eukaryote cell. The structural components shown here are present in organisms as diverse as protozoans, plants, and animals. The nucleus contains the DNA genome and an assembly plant for ribosomal subunits (the nucleolus). The endoplasmic reticulum (ER) and the Golgi work together to modify proteins, most of which are destined for the cell membrane. These proteins travel from the ER to the Golgi and from the Golgi to their final destination in transport vesicles (red and yellow spheres). Mitochondria provide the cell with energy in the form of adenosine triphosphate (ATP). Ribosomes, some of which are attached to the ER, synthesize proteins. Lysosomes and peroxisomes recycle cellular material. The microtubules and centrosome form the spindle apparatus for moving chromosomes to the daughter cells during cell division. Actin and other protein filaments form a weblike cytoskeleton.

tapering to a thin disclike shape at the perimeter. The internal structure is complex, being dominated by a large number of organelles.

The functional organization of a eukaryote is analogous to a
carpentry shop, which is usually divided into two main areas: The
shop floor, where the machinery, building materials, and finishing
rooms are kept, and the shop office, where the work is coordinated
and where the blueprints are stored for everything the shop makes.
Carpentry shops keep a blueprint on file for every item that is made.
When the shop receives an order, perhaps for a chair, someone in
the office makes a copy of the chair's blueprint and delivers it to the
carpenters on the shop floor. In this way, the master copy is kept out
of harm's way, safely stored in the filing cabinet. The carpenters, using the blueprint copy and the materials and tools at hand, build the
chair and then send it into a special room where it is painted. After
the chair is painted, it is taken to another room where it is polished
and then packaged for delivery. The energy for all of this activity
comes through the electrical wires, which are connected to a power
generator somewhere in the local vicinity. The shop communicates
with other shops and its customers by using the telephone, e-mail,
or postal service.

In the cell, the shop floor is called the cytoplasm and the shop
office is the nucleus. Eukaryotes make a large number of proteins
and keep a blueprint for each one, only in this case, the blueprints
are not pictures on pieces of paper but molecules of deoxyribonucleic acid (DNA) that are kept in the nucleus. A cellular blueprint
is called a gene, and a typical cell has thousands of them. A human
cell, for example, has 30,000 genes, all of which are kept on 46 separate DNA molecules known as chromosomes (23 from each parent).
When the cell decides to make a protein it begins by making a ribonucleic acid (RNA) copy of the protein's gene. This blueprint copy,
known as messenger RNA, is made in the nucleus and delivered to
the cell's carpenters in the cytoplasm. These carpenters are enzymes
that control and regulate all of the cell's chemical reactions. Some

of the enzymes are part of a complex protein-synthesizing machine known as a ribosome. Cytoplasmic enzymes and the ribosomes synthesize proteins using mRNA as the template, after which many of the proteins are sent to a compartment known as the endoplasmic reticulum (ER), where they are glycosylated or "painted" with sugar molecules. From there they are shipped to another compartment called the Golgi apparatus where the glycosylation is refined before the finished products, now looking like molecular trees, are loaded into transport bubbles and shipped to their final destination.

The shape of the cell is maintained by an internal cytoskeleton comprised of actin and intermediate filaments. Mitochondria, once free-living prokaryotes, provide the cell with energy in the form of adenosine triphosphate (ATP). The production of ATP is carried out by an assembly of metal-containing proteins, called the electron transport chain, located in the mitochondrion inner membrane. Lysosomes and peroxisomes process and recycle cellular material and molecules. The cell communicates with other cells and the outside world through a forest of glycoproteins, known as the glycocalyx, that covers the cell surface. Producing and maintaining the glycocalyx is the principal function of the ER and Golgi apparatus and a major priority for all eukaryotes.

Cells are biochemical entities that synthesize many thousands of molecules. Studying these chemicals and the biochemistry of the cell would be extremely difficult were it not for the fact that most of the chemical variation is based on six types of molecules that are assembled into just five types of macromolecules. The six basic molecules are amino acids, phosphate, glycerol, sugars, fatty acids, and nucleotides. The five macromolecules are proteins, DNA, RNA, phospholipids, and sugar polymers called polysaccharides.

Molecules of the Cell

Amino acids have a simple core structure consisting of an amino group, a carboxyl group, and a variable R group attached to a

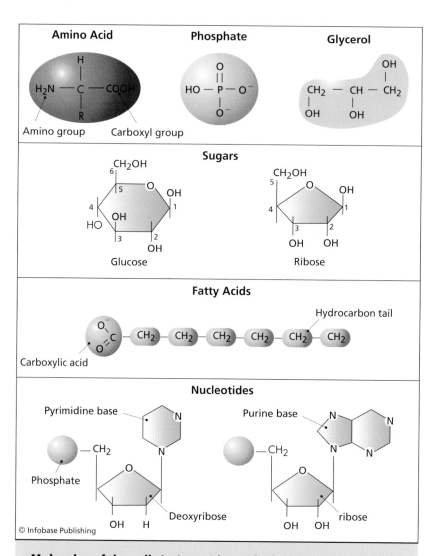

Molecules of the cell. Amino acids are the building blocks for proteins. Phosphate is an important component of many other molecules and is added to proteins to modify their behavior. Glycerol is an alcohol that is an important ingredient in cell membranes and fat. Sugars, like glucose, are a primary energy source for most cells and also have many structural functions. Fatty acids are involved in the production of cell membranes and storage of fat. Nucleotides are the building blocks for DNA and RNA. Note that the sugar carbon atoms are numbered. P: Phosphate; C: Carbon; H: Hydrogen; O: Oxygen; N: Nitrogen; R: Variable molecular group.

carbon atom. There are 20 different kinds of amino acids, each with a unique R group. The simplest and most ancient amino acid is glycine, with an R group that consists only of hydrogen. The chemistry of the various amino acids varies considerably: Some carry a positive electric charge while others are negatively charged or electrically neutral; some are water soluble (hydrophilic) while others are hydrophobic.

Phosphates are extremely important molecules that are used in the construction, or modification, of many other molecules. They are also used to store chemical-bond energy in the form of ATP. The production of phosphate-to-phosphate chemical bonds for use as an energy source is an ancient cellular process, dating back at least 2 billion years.

Glycerol is a simple three-carbon alcohol that is an important component of cell membranes and fat reservoirs. This molecule may have stabilized the membranes of prebiotic bubbles. Interestingly, it is often used today as an ingredient in a solution for making long-lasting soap bubbles.

Sugars are versatile molecules, belonging to a general class of compounds known as carbohydrates that serve a structural role as well as providing energy for the cell. Glucose, a six-carbon sugar, is the primary energy source for most cells and the principal sugar used to glycosylate the proteins and lipids that form the outer coat of all cells. Plants have exploited the structural potential of sugars in their production of cellulose; wood, bark, grasses, and reeds are all polymers of glucose and other monosaccharides. Ribose, a five-carbon sugar, is a component of nucleic acids as well as ATP, the cell's main energy depot. The numbering convention for sugar carbon atoms is shown in the figure on page 160. Ribose carbons are numbered as 1′ (1 prime), 2′, and so on. Consequently, references to nucleic acids, which include ribose, often refer to the 3′ or 5′ carbon.

Fatty acids consist of a carboxyl group (the hydrated form is called carboxylic acid) linked to a hydrophobic hydrocarbon tail.

These molecules are used in the construction of cell membranes and fat. The hydrophobic nature of fatty acids is critically important to the normal function of the cell membrane since it prevents the passive entry of water and water-soluble molecules.

Nucleotides are building blocks for DNA and RNA. These molecules consist of three components: a phosphate, a ribose sugar, and a nitrogenous (nitrogen-containing) ring compound that behaves as a base in solution (a base is a substance that can accept a proton in solution). Nucleotide bases appear in two forms: A single-ring nitrogenous base, called a pyrimidine, and a double-ringed base, called a purine. There are two kinds of purines (adenine and guanine) and three pyrimidines (uracil, cytosine, and thymine). Uracil is specific to RNA, substituting for thymine. In addition, RNA nucleotides contain ribose, whereas DNA nucleotides contain deoxyribose (hence the origin of their names). Ribose has a hydroxyl (OH) group attached to both the 2′ and 3′ carbons, whereas deoxyribose is missing the 2′ hydroxyl group.

Macromolecules of the Cell

The six basic molecules are used by all cells to construct five essential macromolecules: proteins, RNA, DNA, phospholipids, and polysaccharides. Macromolecules have primary, secondary, and tertiary structural levels. The primary structural level refers to the chain that is formed by linking the building blocks together. The secondary structure involves the bending of the linear chain to form a three-dimensional object. Tertiary structural elements involve the formation of chemical bonds between some of the building blocks in the chain to stabilize the secondary structure. A quaternary structure can also occur when two identical molecules interact to form a dimer or double molecule.

Proteins are long chains or polymers of amino acids. The primary structure is held together by peptide bonds that link the carboxyl end of one amino acid to the amino end of a second amino acid. Thus, once constructed, every protein has an amino end and a carboxyl end. An average protein consists of about 400 amino acids.

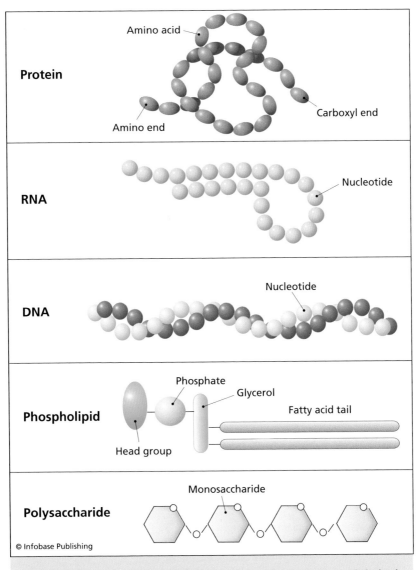

© Infobase Publishing

Macromolecules of the cell. Protein is made from amino acids linked together to form a long chain that can fold up into a three-dimensional structure. RNA and DNA are long chains of nucleotides. RNA is generally single-stranded but can form localized double-stranded regions. DNA is a double-stranded helix with one strand coiling around the other. A phospholipid is composed of a hydrophilic head-group, a phosphate, a glycerol molecule, and two hydrophobic fatty acid tails. Polysaccharides are sugar polymers.

Molecular model of a heat shock protein from the bacterium *Thermoplasma acidophilum.* This protein protects the bacterium from damage by high temperatures. The protein is made up of two chains (red and green). Eight pairs of these chains form a ring, and several rings are stacked to form a tubelike structure. *(Science Source/Photo Researchers, Inc.)*

There are 21 naturally occurring amino acids; with this number the cell can produce an almost infinite variety of proteins. Evolution and natural selection, however, have weeded out most of these, so that eukaryote cells function well with 10,000 to 30,000 different proteins. In addition, this select group of proteins has been conserved over the past 2 billion years (i.e., most of the proteins found in yeast

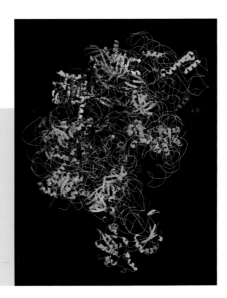

Ribosome protein. Computer model of the structure of a protein from the halophilic (salt-loving) bacterium *Haloarcula marismortui.* The different colors show the different subunits that comprise the protein. *(Protein Data Bank/ Photo Researchers, Inc.)*

can also be found, in modified form, in humans and other higher organisms). The secondary structure of a protein depends on the amino acid sequence and can be quite complicated, often producing three-dimensional structures possessing multiple functions.

RNA is a polymer of the ribonucleotides adenine, uracil, cytosine, and guanine. RNA is generally single-stranded, but it can form localized double-stranded regions by a process known as complementary base pairing, whereby adenine forms a bond with uracil and cytosine pairs with guanine. RNA is involved in the synthesis of proteins and is a structural and enzymatic component of ribosomes.

DNA is a double-stranded nucleic acid. This macromolecule encodes cellular genes and is constructed from adenine, thymine, cytosine, and guanine deoxyribonucleotides. The two DNA strands coil around each other like strands in a piece of rope, creating a double helix. The two strands are complementary throughout the length of the molecule: adenine pairs with thymine and cytosine pairs with guanine. Thus, if the sequence of one strand is known to be ATCGTC, the sequence of the other strand must be TAGCAG.

Phospholipids are the main component in cell membranes. These macromolecules are composed of a polar head group (usually an alcohol), a phosphate, glycerol, and two hydrophobic fatty acid tails. Fat that is stored in the body as an energy reserve has a structure similar to a phospholipid, being composed of three fatty acid chains attached to a molecule of glycerol. The third fatty acid takes the place of the phosphate and head group of a phospholipid.

Polysaccharides are sugar polymers consisting of two or more monosaccharides. Disaccharides (two monosaccharides) and oligosaccharides (about three to 12 monosaccharides) are attached to proteins and lipids destined for the cell surface or the extracellular matrix. Polysaccharides, such as glycogen and starch, may contain several hundred monosaccharides and are stored in cells as an energy reserve.

Basic Cellular Functions

There are six basic cellular functions: DNA replication, DNA maintenance, gene expression, power generation, cell division, and cell communication. DNA replication usually occurs in conjunction with cell division, but there are exceptions known as polyploidization (see glossary). Gene expression refers to the process whereby the information stored in a gene is used to synthesize RNA or protein. The production of power is accomplished by extracting energy from food molecules and then storing that energy in a form that is readily available to the cell. Cells communicate with their environment and with other cells. The communication hardware consists of a variety of special macromolecules that are embedded in the cell membrane.

DNA Replication

Replication is made possible by the complementarity of the two DNA strands. Since adenine (A) always pairs with thymine (T) and guanine (G) always pairs with cytosine (C), replication enzymes are able to duplicate the molecule by treating each of the original strands as templates for the new strands. For example, if a portion of the template strand reads ATCGTTGC, the new strand will be TAGCAACG.

DNA replication requires the coordinated effort of a team of enzymes, led by DNA helicase and primase. The helicase separates the two DNA strands at the astonishing rate of 1,000 nucleotides every second. This enzyme gets its name from the fact that it unwinds the DNA helix as it separates the two strands. The enzyme that is directly responsible for reading the template strand and for synthesizing the new daughter strand is called DNA polymerase. This enzyme also has an editorial function; it checks the preceding nucleotide to make sure it is correct before it adds a nucleotide to the growing chain. The editor function of this enzyme introduces an interesting problem. How can the polymerase add the very first nucleotide when it has to check a preceding nucleotide before adding a new one? A special enzyme, called primase, which is attached to the helicase, solves this problem. Primase synthesizes short pieces of RNA that form a DNA-RNA double-stranded region. The RNA becomes a temporary part of the daughter strand, thus priming the DNA polymerase by providing the crucial first nucleotide in the new strand. Once the chromosome is duplicated, DNA repair enzymes, discussed below, remove the RNA primers and replace them with DNA nucleotides.

DNA Maintenance

Every day in a typical human cell thousands of nucleotides are being damaged by spontaneous chemical events, environmental pollutants, and radiation. In many cases, it takes only a single defective nucleotide within the coding region of a gene to produce an inactive, mutant protein. The most common forms of DNA damage are depurination and deamination. Depurination is the loss of a purine base (guanine or adenine) resulting in a gap in the DNA sequence, referred to as a missing tooth. Deamination converts cytosine to uracil, a base that is normally found only in RNA.

About 5,000 purines are lost from each human cell every day, and over the same time period 100 cytosines are deaminated per cell. Depurination and deamination produce a great deal of damage, and in either case the daughter strand ends up with a missing nucleotide and possibly a mutated gene, as the DNA replication machinery simply bypasses the uracil or the missing tooth. If left unrepaired, the mutated genes will be passed on to all daughter cells, with catastrophic consequences for the organism as a whole.

DNA damage caused by depurination is repaired by special nuclear proteins that detect the missing tooth, excise about 10 nucleotides on either side of the damage, and then, using the complementary strand as a guide, reconstruct the strand correctly. Deamination is dealt with by a special group of DNA repair enzymes known as base-flippers. These enzymes inspect the DNA one nucleotide at a time. After binding to a nucleotide, a base-flipper breaks the hydrogen bonds holding the nucleotide to its complementary partner. It then performs the maneuver for which it gets its name. Holding on to the nucleotide, it rotates the base a full 180 degrees, inspects it carefully, and, if it detects any damage, cuts the base out and discards it. In this case, the base-flipper leaves the final repair to the missing-tooth crew that detects and repairs the gap as described previously. If the nucleotide is normal, the base-flipper rotates it back into place and reseals the hydrogen bonds. Scientists have estimated that these maintenance crews inspect and repair the entire genome of a typical human cell in less than 24 hours.

Gene Expression

Genes encode proteins and several kinds of RNA. Extracting the coded information from DNA requires two sequential processes known as transcription and translation. A gene is said to be expressed when either or both of these processes have been completed. Transcription, catalyzed by the enzyme RNA polymerase, copies one strand of the DNA into a complementary strand of mRNA, which is sent to the cytoplasm where it joins with a ribosome. Translation is a process that is orchestrated by the ribosomes. These particles synthesize proteins using mRNA and the genetic code as guides. The ribosome can synthesize any protein specified by the mRNA and the mRNA can be translated many times before it is recycled. Some RNAs, such as ribosomal RNA and transfer RNA are never translated. Ribosomal RNA (rRNA) is a structural and enzymatic component of ribosomes. Transfer RNA (tRNA), though separate from the ribosome, is part of the translation machinery.

The genetic code provides a way for the translation machinery to interpret the sequence information stored in the DNA molecule and represented by mRNA. DNA is a linear sequence of four different kinds of nucleotides, so the simplest code could be one in which each nucleotide specifies a different amino acid; that is, adenine coding for the amino acid glycine, cytosine for lysine, and so on. The earliest cells may have used this coding system, but it is limited to the construction of proteins consisting of only four different kinds of amino acids. Eventually, a more elaborate code evolved in which a combination of three out of the four possible DNA nucleotides, called codons, specifies a single amino acid. With this scheme, it is possible to have a unique code for each of the 20 naturally occurring amino acids. For example, the codon AGC specifies the amino acid serine, whereas TGC specifies the amino acid cysteine. Thus, a gene may be viewed as a long continuous sequence of codons. However, not all codons specify an amino acid. The sequence TGA signals the end of the gene and a special codon ATG signals the start site, in addition to specifying the amino acid methionine. Consequently, all proteins begin with this amino acid, although it is sometimes re-moved once construction of the protein is complete. As mentioned above, an average protein may consist of 300 to 400 amino acids; since the codon consists of three nucleotides for each amino acid, a typical gene may be 900 to 1,200 nucleotides long.

Power Generation

Dietary fats, sugars, and proteins, not targeted for growth, storage, or repairs, are converted to ATP by the mitochondria. This process requires a number of metal-binding proteins called the respiratory chain (also known as the electron transport chain) and a special ion channel enzyme called ATP synthase. The respiratory chain consists of three major components: NADH dehydrogenase, cytochrome b, and cytochrome oxidase. All of these components are protein complexes with an iron (NADH dehydrogenase, cytochrome b) or a copper core (cytochrome oxidase) and, together with the ATP syn-thase, are located in the inner membrane of the mitochondria.

The respiratory chain is analogous to an electric cable that trans-ports electricity from a hydroelectric dam to our homes, where it is used to turn on lights or run our stereos. The human body, like that of all animals, generates electricity by processing food molecules through a metabolic pathway called the Krebs cycle, also located within the mitochondria. The electrons (electricity) so generated are transferred to hydrogen ions, which quickly bind to a special nucleotide called nicotinamide adenine dinucleotide (NAD). Binding of the hydrogen ion to NAD is noted by abbreviating the resulting molecule as NADH. The electrons begin their journey down the respiratory chain when NADH binds to NADH dehydrogenase, the first component in the chain. This enzyme does just what its name implies: It removes the hydrogen from NADH, releasing the stored electrons, which are conducted through the chain by the iron and copper as though they were traveling along an electric wire. As the electrons travel from one end of the chain to the other they energize the synthesis of ATP, which is released from the mitochondria for use by the cell. All electrical circuits must have a ground, that is, the electrons need someplace to go once they have completed the circuit. In the case of the respiratory chain, the ground is oxygen. After passing through cytochrome oxidase, the last component in the chain, the electrons are picked up by oxygen, which combines with hydrogen ions to form water.

The Cell Cycle

Free-living single cells divide as a way of reproducing their kind. Among plants and animals, cells divide as the organism grows from a seed or an embryo into a mature individual. This form of cell division, in which the parent cell divides into two identical daughter cells, is called mitosis. A second form of cell division, known as meiosis, is intended for sexual reproduction and occurs exclusively in gonads.

Cell division is part of a grander process known as the cell cycle, which consists of two phases: interphase and M phase (meiosis or mitosis). Interphase is divided into three subphases called Gap 1 (G_1), S phase (a period of DNA synthesis), and Gap 2 (G_2). The con-

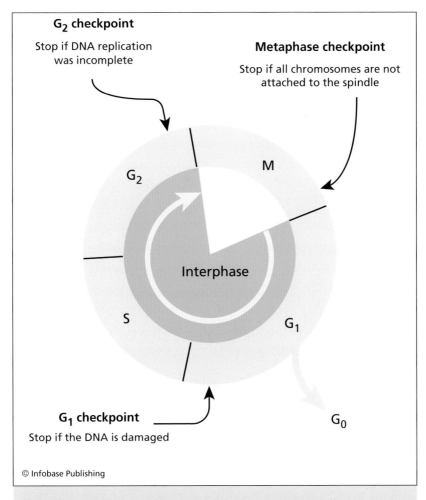

The cell cycle. Many cells spend their time cycling between interphase and M phase (cell division by mitosis or meiosis). Interphase is divided into three subphases: Gap 1(G_1), S phase (DNA synthesis), and Gap 2 (G_2). Cells may exit the cycle by entering G_0. The cell cycle is equipped with three checkpoints to ensure the daughter cells are identical and that there is no genetic damage. The yellow arrow indicates the direction of the cycle.

clusion of interphase, and with it the termination of G_2, occurs with division of the cell and a return to G_1. Cells may leave the cycle by entering a special phase called G_0. Some cells, such as post-mitotic neurons in an animal's brain, remain in G_0 for the life of the organism. For most cells, the completion of the cycle, known as the generation time, can take 30 to 60 minutes.

Cells grow continuously during interphase while preparing for the next round of division. Two notable events are the duplication of the spindle (the centrosome and associated microtubules), a structure that is crucial for the movement of the chromosomes during cell division, and the appearance of an enzyme called maturation promoting factor (MPF) at the end of G_2. MPF phosphorylates histones, proteins that bind to the DNA, and when phosphorylated compact (or condense) the chromosomes in preparation for cell division. MPF is also responsible for the breakdown of the nuclear membrane. When cell division is complete, MPF disappears, allowing the chromosomes to decondense and the nuclear envelope to reform. Completion of a normal cell cycle always involves the division of a cell into two daughter cells, either meiotically or mitotically.

Cell division is such a complex process that many things can, and do, go wrong. Cell cycle monitors, consisting of a team of enzymes, check to make sure that everything is going well each time a cell divides, and if it is not, those monitors stop the cell from dividing until the problem is corrected. If the damage cannot be repaired, a cell remains stuck in midstream for the remainder of its life. If this happens to a cell in an animal's body, it is forced to commit suicide, in a process called apoptosis, by other cells in the immediate neighborhood or by the immune system.

The cell cycle includes three checkpoints: the first is a DNA damage checkpoint that occurs in G_1. The monitors check for damage that may have occurred as a result of the last cell cycle or were caused by something in the environment, such as UV radiation or toxic chemicals. If damage is detected, DNA synthesis is blocked until it can be repaired. The second checkpoint occurs in G_2, where the monitors make sure errors were not introduced when the chromosomes were duplicated during S phase. The G_1 and G_2 checkpoints are sometimes referred to collectively as DNA damage checkpoints. The third and final checkpoint occurs in M phase, to ensure that all of the chromosomes are properly attached to the spindle. This checkpoint is intended to prevent gross abnormalities in the daughter cells with regard to chromosome number. If a chromosome fails to attach to the spindle, one daughter cell will end up with too many chromosomes, while the other will have too few.

Mitosis

Mitosis is divided into four stages known as prophase, metaphase, anaphase, and telophase. The behavior and movement of the chromosomes characterize each stage. At prophase, DNA replication has already occurred and the nuclear membrane begins to break down. Condensation of the duplicated chromosomes initiates the phase (i.e., the very long, thin chromosomes are folded up to produce short thick chromosomes that are easy to move and maneuver). Under the microscope, the chromosomes become visible as X-shaped structures, which are the two duplicated chromosomes, often called sister chromatids. A special region of each chromosome, called a centromere, holds the chromatids together. Proteins bind to the centromere to form a structure called the kinetochore. The centrosome is duplicated, and the two migrate to opposite ends of the cell.

During metaphase, the chromosomes are sorted out and aligned between the two centrosomes. By this time, the nuclear membrane has completely broken down. The two centrosomes and the microtubules fanning out between them form the mitotic spindle. The area in between the spindles, where the chromosomes are aligned, is known as the metaphase plate. Some of the microtubules make contact with the kinetochores, while others overlap, with motor proteins situated in between.

Anaphase begins when the duplicated chromosomes move to opposite poles of the cell. The first step is the release of an enzyme that breaks the bonds holding the kinetochores together, thus allowing the sister chromatids to separate from each other while remaining bound to their respective microtubules. Motor proteins, using energy supplied by ATP, move along the microtubule dragging the chromosomes to opposite ends of the cell.

During telophase, the daughter chromosomes arrive at the spindle poles and decondense to form the relaxed chromosomes characteristic of interphase nuclei. The nuclear envelope begins forming around the chromosomes, marking the end of mitosis. By the end of telophase, individual chromosomes are no longer distinguishable and are referred to as chromatin. While the nuclear membrane reforms, a contractile ring, made of the proteins myosin and actin, begins pinching the parental cell in two. This stage, separate from mitosis, is called cytokinesis and leads to the formation of two daughter cells, each with one nucleus.

Meiosis

Many eukaryotes reproduce sexually through the fusion of gametes (eggs and sperm). If gametes were produced mitotically, a catastrophic growth in the number of chromosomes would occur each time a sperm fertilized an egg. Meiosis is a special form of cell division that prevents this from happening by producing haploid gametes, each possessing half as many chromosomes as the diploid cell. When haploid gametes fuse, they produce an embryo with the correct number of chromosomes.

Unlike mitosis, which produces two identical daughter cells, meiosis produces four genetically unique daughter cells that have half the number of chromosomes found in the parent cell. This is possible because meiosis consists of two rounds of cell division, called meiosis I and meiosis II, with only one round of DNA synthesis. Microbiologists discovered meiosis almost 100 years ago by comparing the number of chromosomes in somatic cells and germ cells. The roundworm, for example, was found to have four chromosomes in its somatic cells, but only two in its gametes. Many other studies also compared the amount of DNA in nuclei from somatic cells and gonads, always with the same result: The amount of DNA in somatic cells is at least double the amount in fully mature gametes.

Meiotic divisions are divided into the four mitotic stages discussed above. Indeed, meiosis II is virtually identical to a mitotic division. Meiosis I resembles mitosis, but close examination shows two important differences: gene swapping occurs between homologous chromosomes in prophase, producing recombinant chromosomes and the distribution of maternal and paternal chromosomes to different daughter cells. At the end of meiosis I, one of the daughter cells contains a mixture of normal and recombinant maternal chromosomes and the other contains normal and recombinant paternal chromosomes. During meiosis II, the duplicated chromosomes are distributed to different daughter cells, yielding four genetically unique cells: paternal, paternal recombinant, maternal, and maternal recombinant. Mixing genetic material in this way is unique to meiosis, and it is one of the reasons sexual reproduction has been such a powerful evolutionary force.

Cell Communication

A forest of glycoproteins and glycolipids covers the surface of every cell like trees on the surface of the Earth. The cell's forest is called the glycocalyx, and many of its trees function like sensory antennae. Cells use these antennae to communicate with their environment and with other cells. In multicellular organisms, the glycocalyx also plays an important role in holding cells together. In this case, the antennae of adjacent cells are connected to each other through the formation of chemical bonds.

The sensory antennae, also known as receptors, are linked to a variety of secondary molecules that serve to relay messages to the interior of the cell. These molecules, some of which are called second messengers, may activate machinery in the cytoplasm or they may enter the nucleus to activate gene expression. The signals that a cell receives are of many different kinds but generally fall into one of five categories: 1) proliferation, which stimulates the cell to grow and divide; 2) activation, which is a request for the cell to synthesize and release specific molecules; 3) deactivation, which serves as a brake for a previous activation signal; 4) navigation, which helps direct the cell to a specific location (This is very important for free-living cells hunting for food and for immune system cells that are hunting for invading microorganisms); and 5) termination, which is a signal that orders the cell to commit suicide. This death signal occurs during embryonic development (e.g., the loss of webbing between the fingers and toes) and during an infection. In some cases, the only way the immune system can deal with an invading pathogenic microbe is to order some of the infected cells to commit suicide. This process is known as apoptosis.

BIOTECHNOLOGY

Biotechnology (also known as recombinant DNA technology) consists of several procedures that are used to study the structure and function of genes and their products. Central to this technology is the ability to clone specific pieces of DNA and to construct libraries of these DNA fragments that represent the genetic repertoire of an entire organism or a specific cell type. With these libraries at hand, scientists have been able to study the cell and whole organisms in unprecedented detail. The information so gained has revolutionized biology as well as many other disciplines, including medical science, pharmacology, psychiatry, and anthropology, to name but a few.

DNA Cloning

In 1973, scientists discovered that restriction enzymes (enzymes that can cut DNA at specific sites), DNA ligase (an enzyme that can join two pieces of DNA together), and bacterial plasmids could be used to clone DNA molecules. Plasmids are small (about 3,000 base pairs) circular minichromosomes that occur naturally in bacteria and are

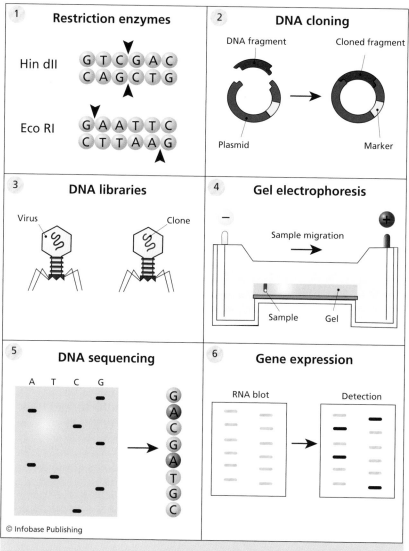

1 Restriction enzymes

Hin dII   G T C G A C
           C A G C T G

Eco RI   G A A T T C
          C T T A A G

2 DNA cloning

DNA fragment   Cloned fragment

Plasmid   Marker

3 DNA libraries

Virus   Clone

4 Gel electrophoresis

−   +

Sample migration

Sample   Gel

5 DNA sequencing

A   T   C   G

G
A
C
G
A
T
G
C

© Infobase Publishing

6 Gene expression

RNA blot   Detection

Biotechnology. This technology consists of six basic steps: 1) digestion of DNA with restriction enzymes in order to isolate specific DNA fragments; 2) cloning of restriction fragments in circular bacterial minichromosomes to increase their numbers; 3) storing the fragments for further study in viral-based DNA libraries; 4) isolation and purification of DNA fragments from gene libraries using gel electrophoresis; 5) sequencing cloned DNA fragments; and 6) determining the expression profile of selected DNA clones using RNA blots and radioactive detection procedures.

often exchanged between cells by passive diffusion. A bacterium is said to be transfected when it acquires a new plasmid. For bacteria, the main advantage to swapping plasmids is that they often carry antibiotic resistance genes, so that a cell sensitive to ampicillin can become resistant simply by acquiring the right plasmid. For scientists, plasmid-swapping provided an ideal method for amplifying or cloning a specific piece of DNA.

The first cloning experiment used a plasmid from the bacterium *Escherichia coli* that was cut with the restriction enzyme *Eco*RI. The plasmid had a single *Eco*RI site so the restriction enzyme simply opened the circular molecule. Foreign DNA, cut with the same restriction enzyme, was incubated with the plasmid. Because the plasmid and foreign DNA were both cut with *Eco*RI, the DNA could insert itself into the plasmid to form a hybrid, or recombinant plasmid, after which DNA ligase sealed the two together. The reaction mixture was added to a small volume of *E. coli* so that some of the cells could take up the recombinant plasmid before being transferred to a nutrient broth containing streptomycin. Only those cells carrying the recombinant plasmid, which contained an anti-streptomycin gene, could grow in the presence of this antibiotic. Each time the cells divided, the plasmid DNA was duplicated along with the main chromosome. After the cells had grown overnight, the foreign DNA had been amplified billions of times and was easily isolated for sequencing or expression studies. In this procedure, the plasmid is known as a cloning vector because it serves to transfer the foreign DNA into a cell.

DNA Libraries

The basic cloning procedure described above not only provides a way to amplify a specific piece of DNA but can also be used to construct DNA libraries. In this case, however, the cloning vector is a bacteriophage called lambda. The lambda genome is double-stranded DNA of about 40,000 base pairs (bp), much of which can be replaced by foreign DNA without sacrificing the ability of the virus to infect bacteria. This is the great advantage of lambda over a plasmid. Lambda can accommodate very long pieces of DNA, often long enough to contain an entire gene, whereas a plasmid cannot accommodate foreign DNA that is larger than 2,000 bps. Moreover, bacteriophage has the natural ability to infect bacteria, so that the efficiency of transfection is 100 times greater than it is for plasmids.

The construction of a DNA library begins with the isolation of genomic DNA and its digestion with a restriction enzyme to produce fragments of 1,000 to 10,000 bp. These fragments are ligated into lambda genomes, which are subjected to a packaging reaction to produce mature viral particles, most of which carry a different piece of the genomic DNA. This collection of viruses is called a genomic library and is used to study the structure and organization of specific genes. Clones from a library such as this contain the coding sequences, in addition to noncoding sequences such as introns, intervening sequences, promoters, and enhancers. An alternative form of a DNA library can be constructed by isolating mRNA from a specific cell type. This RNA is converted to the complimentary DNA (cDNA) using an RNA-dependent DNA polymerase called reverse transcriptase. The cDNA is ligated to lambda genomes and packaged as for the genomic library. This collection of recombinant viruses is known as a cDNA library and contains genes that were being expressed by the cells when the mRNA was extracted. It does not include introns or controlling elements as these are lost during transcription and the processing that occurs in the cell to make mature mRNA. Thus a cDNA library is intended for the purpose of studying gene expression and the structure of the coding region only.

Labeling Cloned DNA

Many of the procedures used in biotechnology were inspired by the events that occur during DNA replication (described above). This includes the labeling of cloned DNA for use as probes in expression studies, DNA sequencing, and polymerase chain reaction (PCR) that is described below. DNA replication involves duplicating one of the strands (the parent, or template strand) by linking nucleotides in an order specified by the template and depends on a large number of enzymes, the most important of which is DNA polymerase. This enzyme, guided by the template strand, constructs a daughter strand by linking nucleotides together. One such nucleotide is deoxyadenine triphosphate (dATP). Deoxyribonucleotides have a single hydroxyl group located at the 3′ carbon of the sugar group while the triphosphate is attached to the 5′ carbon.

The procedure for labeling DNA probes, developed in 1983, introduces radioactive nucleotides into a DNA molecule. This method supplies DNA polymerase with a single-stranded DNA template, a primer, and the four nucleotides in a buffered solution to induce in vitro replication. The daughter strand, which becomes the labeled probe, is made radioactive by including a ^{32}P-labeled nucleotide in the reaction mix. The radioactive nucleotide is usually deoxycytidine triphosphate (dCTP) or dATP. The ^{32}P is always part of the α phosphate (the phosphate closest to the 5′ carbon), as this is the one used by the polymerase to form the phosphodiester bond between nucleotides. Nucleotides can also be labeled with a fluorescent dye molecule.

Single-stranded DNA hexamers (six bases long) are used as primers, and these are produced in such a way that they contain all possible permutations of four bases taken six at a time. Randomizing the base sequence for the primers ensures that there will be at least one primer site in a template that is only 50 bp long. Templates used in labeling reactions such as this are generally 100 to 800 bp long. This strategy of labeling DNA is known as random primer labeling.

Gel Electrophoresis

This procedure is used to separate DNA and RNA fragments by size in a slab of agarose (highly refined agar) or polyacrylamide subjected to an electric field. Nucleic acids carry a negative charge and thus will migrate toward a positively charged electrode. The gel acts as a sieving medium that impedes the movement of the molecules. Thus, the rate at which the fragments migrate is a function of their size; small fragments migrate more rapidly than large fragments. The gel, containing the samples, is run submerged in a special pH-regulated solution, or buffer. Agarose gels are run horizontally as shown in the figure on page 177. But DNA-sequencing gels, made of polyacrylamide, are much bigger and are run in a vertical tank.

DNA Sequencing

A sequencing reaction developed by the British biochemist Dr. Fred Sanger in 1976 is a technique that takes its inspiration from the natural process of DNA replication. DNA polymerase requires a primer with a free 3′ hydroxyl group. The polymerase adds the first nucleotide to this group, and all subsequent bases are added to the 3′ hydroxyl of the previous base. Sequencing by the Sanger method is usually performed with the DNA cloned into a special sequencing plasmid. This simplifies the choice of the primers since their sequence can be derived from the known plasmid sequence. Once the primer binds to the primer site the cloned DNA may be replicated.

Sanger's innovation involved the synthesis of chain-terminating nucleotide analogues lacking the 3′ hydroxyl group. These analogues, also known as dideoxynucleotides (ddATP, ddCTP, ddGTP, and ddTTP), terminate the growth of the daughter strand at the point of insertion, and this can be used to determine the distance of each base on the daughter strand from the primer. These distances can be visualized by separating the Sanger reaction products on a polyacrylamide gel and then exposing the gel to X-ray film to produce an autoradiogram. The DNA sequence is read directly from this film beginning with the smallest fragment at the bottom of the gel (the nucleotide closest to the primer) and ending with the largest fragment at the top. A hypothetical autoradiogram and the derived DNA sequence are shown in panel 5 of the figure on page 177. The smallest fragment in this example is the C nucleotide at the bottom of lane 3. The next nucleotide in the sequence is the G nucleotide in lane 4, then the T nucleotide in lane 2, and so on to the top of the gel.

Automated versions of the Sanger sequencing reaction use fluorescent-labeled dideoxynucleotides, each with a different color, so the sequence of the template can be recorded by a computer as the reaction mix passes a sensitive photocell. Machines such as this were used to sequence the human genome—a job that cost many millions of dollars and took years to complete. Recent advances in DNA-sequencing technology will make it possible to sequence the human genome in less than a week at a cost of $1,000.

Gene Expression

The production of a genomic or cDNA library, followed by the sequencing of isolated clones, is a very powerful method for characterizing genes and the genomes from which they came. But the icing on the cake is the ability to determine the expression profile for a gene—that is, to determine which cells express the gene and exactly when the gene is turned on and off. Typical experiments may wish to determine the expression of specific genes in normal versus cancerous tissue or tissues obtained from groups of different ages. There are essentially three methods for doing this: RNA blotting, fluorescent in situ hybridization (FISH), and the polymerase chain reaction (PCR).

RNA Blotting

This procedure consists of the following steps:

1. Extract mRNA from the cells or tissue of interest.
2. Fractionate (separate by size) the mRNA sample using gel electrophoresis.

3. Transfer the fractionated sample to a nylon membrane (the blotting step).
4. Incubate the membrane with a gene fragment (usually a cDNA clone) that has been labeled with a radioisotope.
5. Expose the membrane to X-ray film to visualize the signal.

The RNA is transferred from the gel to a nylon membrane using a vacuum apparatus or a simple dish containing a transfer buffer topped by a large stack of ordinary paper towels and a weight. The paper towels pull the transfer buffer through the gel, eluting the RNA from the gel and trapping it on the membrane. The location of specific mRNAs can be determined by hybridizing the membrane to a radiolabeled cDNA or genomic clone. The hybridization procedure involves placing the membrane in a buffer solution containing a labeled probe. During a long incubation period, the probe binds to the target sequence immobilized on the membrane. A-T and G-C base pairing (also known as hybridization) mediate the binding between the probe and target. The double-stranded molecule that is formed is a hybrid, being formed between the RNA target, on the membrane, and the DNA probe.

Fluorescent In Situ Hybridization

Studying gene expression does not always depend on RNA blots and membrane hybridization. In the 1980s, scientists found that cDNA probes could be hybridized to DNA or RNA in situ, that is, while located within cells or tissue sections fixed on a microscope slide. In this case, the probe is labeled with a fluorescent dye molecule, rather than a radioactive isotope. The samples are then examined and photographed under a fluorescent microscope. FISH is an extremely powerful variation on RNA blotting. This procedure gives precise information regarding the identity of a cell that expresses a specific gene, information that usually cannot be obtained with membrane hybridization. Organs and tissues are generally composed of many different kinds of cells, which cannot be separated from each other using standard biochemical extraction procedures. Histological sections, however, show clearly the various cell types and, when subjected to FISH analysis, provide clear information as to which cells express specific genes. FISH is also used in clinical laboratories for the diagnosis of genetic abnormalities.

Polymerase Chain Reaction

PCR is simply repetitive DNA replication over a limited, primer-defined region of a suitable template. It provides a way of amplifying a short segment of DNA without going through the cloning procedures described above. The region defined by the primers is amplified to such an extent that it can be easily isolated for further study. The reaction exploits the fact that a DNA duplex, in a low salt buffer, will melt (i.e., separate into two single strands) at 167°F (75°C), but will re-anneal (rehybridize) at 98.6°F (37°C).

The reaction is initiated by melting the template, in the presence of primers and polymerase in a suitable buffer, cooling quickly to 98.6°F (37°C), and allowing sufficient time for the polymerase to replicate both strands of the template. The temperature is then increased to 167°F (75°C) to melt the newly formed duplexes and then cooled to 98.6°F (37°C). At the lower temperature, more primer will anneal to initiate another round of replication. The heating-cooling cycle is repeated 20 to 30 times, after which the reaction products are fractionated on an agarose gel and the region containing the amplified fragment is cut out of the gel and purified for further study. The DNA polymerase used in these reactions is isolated from thermophilic bacteria that can withstand temperatures of 158°F (70°C) to 176°F (80°C). PCR applications are nearly limitless. PCR is used to amplify DNA from samples containing, at times, no more than a few cells. It is being used in the development of ultrafast DNA sequencers, identification of tissue samples in criminal investigations, amplification of ancient DNA obtained from fossils, and the identification of genes that are turned on or off during embryonic development or during cellular transformation (cancer formation).

GENE AND PROTEIN NOMENCLATURE

Scientists who were, in effect, probing around in the dark have discovered many genes and their encoded proteins. Once discovered, the new genes or proteins had to be named. Usually the "name" is nothing more than a lab-book code or an acronym suggested by the system under study at the time. Sometimes it turns out, after further study, that the function observed in the original study is a minor aspect of the gene's role in the cell. It is for this reason that gene and protein names sometimes seem absurd and poorly chosen.

In 2003, an International Committee on Standardized Genetic Nomenclature agreed to unify the rules and guidelines for gene and protein names for the mouse and rat. Similar committees have attempted to standardize gene-naming conventions for human, frog, zebrafish, and yeast genes. In general, the gene name is expected to be brief and to begin with a lowercase letter unless it is a person's name. The gene symbols are acronyms taken from the gene name and are expected to be three to five characters long and not more than 10. The symbols must be written with Roman letters and Arabic numbers. The same symbol is used for orthologs (i.e., the same gene) among different species, such as human, mouse, or rat. Thus the gene sonic hedgehog is symbolized as shh and the gene myelocytomatosis is symbolized as myc.

Unfortunately, the various committees were unable to agree on a common presentation for the gene and protein symbols. A human gene symbol, for example, is italicized, uppercase letters and the protein is uppercase and not italicized. A frog gene symbol is lowercase and the protein is uppercase, while neither is italicized. Thus the myc gene and its protein, for example, are written as *MYC* and

MYC in humans, myc and MYC in frogs, and *Myc* and Myc in mice and rats. The latter convention, *Myc* and Myc, is used throughout the New Biology set, regardless of the species.

WEIGHTS AND MEASURES

The following table presents some common weights, measures, and conversions that appear in this book and other volumes of the New Biology set.

QUANTITY	EQUIVALENT
Length	1 meter (m) = 100 centimeters (cm) = 1.094 yards = 39.37 inches 1 kilometer (km) = 1000 m = 0.62 miles 1 foot = 30.48 cm 1 inch = 1/12 foot = 2.54 cm 1 cm = 0.394 inch = 10^{-2} (or 0.01) m 1 millimeter (mm) = 10^{-3} m 1 micrometer (μm) = 10^{-6} m 1 nanometer (nm) = 10^{-9} m 1 Ångström (Å) = 10^{-10} m
Mass	1 gram (g) = 0.0035 ounce 1 pound = 16 ounces = 453.6 grams 1 kilogram (kg) = 2.2 pounds (lb) 1 milligram (mg) = 10^{-3} g 1 microgram (μg) = 10^{-6} g
Volume	1 liter (l) = 1.06 quarts (U.S.) = 0.264 gallon (U.S.) 1 quart (U.S.) = 32 fluid ounces = 0.95 liter 1 milliliter (ml) = 10^{-3} liter = 1 cubic centimeter (cc)
Temperature	°C = 5/9 (°F - 32) °F = (9/5 × °C) + 32

Energy	Calorie = the amount of heat needed to raise the
	     temperature of 1 gram of water by 1°C.
	Kilocalorie = 1,000 calories. Used to describe the energy
	     content of foods.

 # Glossary

acetyl   A chemical group derived from acetic acid. Important in energy metabolism and for the modification of proteins.

acetyl-CoA   A water-soluble molecule, coenzyme A (CoA) that carries acetyl groups in cells.

acetylcholine   A neurotransmitter released at axonal terminals by cholinergic neurons. Found in the central and peripheral nervous system, and is released at the vertebrate neuromuscular junction.

acid   A substance that releases protons when dissolved in water. Carries a net negative charge.

actin filament   A protein filament formed by the polymerization of globular actin molecules. Forms the cytoskeleton of all eucaryotes and part of the contractile apparatus of skeletal muscle.

action potential   A self-propagating electrical impulse that occurs in the membranes of neurons, muscles, photoreceptors, and hair cells of the inner ear.

active transport   Movement of molecules across the cell membrane, utilizing the energy stored in ATP.

adenylate cyclase   A membrane-bound enzyme that catalyzes the conversion of ATP to cyclic AMP. An important component of cell signaling pathways.

adherens junction   A cell junction in which the cytoplasmic face of the membrane is attached to actin filaments

adipocyte   A fat cell.

adrenaline (epinephrine)   A hormone released by chromaffin cells in the adrenal gland. Prepares an animal for extreme activity, increases the heart rate and blood sugar levels.

adult stem cells   Stem cells isolated from adult tissues, such as bone marrow or epithelium.

aerobic   Refers to a process that either requires oxygen or occurs in its presence.

agar   A polysaccharide isolated from sea weed that forms a gel when boiled in water and cooled to room temperature. Used by microbiologists as a solid culture medium for the isolation and growth of bacteria and fungi.

agarose   A purified form of agar that is used to fractionate (separate by size) biomolecules.

allele   An alternate form of a gene. Diploid organisms have two alleles for each gene, located at the same locus (position) on homologous chromosomes.

alpha helix   A common folding pattern of proteins in which a linear sequence of amino acids twists into a right-handed helix stabilized by hydrogen bonds.

allogeneic transplant   A cell, tissue, or organ transplant from an unrelated individual.

amino acid   An organic molecule containing amino and carboxyl groups that is a building block of protein.

aminoacyl-tRNA synthetase   An enzyme that attaches the correct amino acid to a tRNA.

amino terminus   The end of a protein or polypeptide chain that carries a free amino group.

aminoacyl tRNA   An amino acid linked by its carboxyl group to a hydroxyl group on tRNA.

amphipathic   Having both hydrophilic and hydrophobic regions, as in a phospholipid.

anabolism   A collection of metabolic reactions in a cell whereby large molecules are made from smaller ones.

anaerobic   A cellular metabolism that does not depend on molecular oxygen.

anaphase   A mitotic stage in which the two sets of chromosomes move away from each other towards opposite spindle poles.

anchoring junction   A cell junction that attaches cells to each other.

angiogenesis   Sprouting of new blood vessels from preexisting ones.

angstrom   A unit of length, equal to 10^{-10} meter or 0.1 nanometer (nM), that is used to measure molecules and atoms.

anterior   A position close to or at the head end of the body.

antibiotic   A substance made by bacteria, fungi, and plants that is toxic to microorganisms. Common examples are penicillin and streptomycin.

antibody   A protein made by B cells of the immune system in response to invading microbes.

anticodon   A sequence of three nucleotides in tRNA that is complementary to a messenger RNA codon.

antigen   A molecule that stimulates an immune response, leading to the formation of antibodies.

antigen-presenting cell   A cell of the immune system, such as a monocyte, that presents pieces of an invading microbe (the antigen) to lymphocytes.

antiparallel   The relative orientation of the two strands in a DNA double helix; the polarity of one strand is oriented in the opposite direction to the other.

antiporter   A membrane carrier protein that transports two different molecules across a membrane in opposite directions.

apoptosis   Regulated or programmed form of cell death that may be activated by the cell itself or by the immune system to force cells to commit suicide when they become infected with a virus or bacterium.

archaea   The archaea are prokaryotes that are physically similar to bacteria (both lack a nucleus and internal organelles), but they have retained a primitive biochemistry and physiology that would have been commonplace 2 billion years ago.

asexual reproduction   The process of forming new individuals without gametes or the fertilization of an egg by a sperm. Individuals produced this way are identical to the parent and referred to as a clone.

aster   The star-shaped arrangement of microtubules that is characteristic of a mitotic or meiotic spindle.

ATP (adenosine triphosphate)   A nucleoside consisting of adenine, ribose, and three phosphate groups that is the main carrier of chemical energy in the cell.

ATP synthase   A protein located in the inner membrane of the mitochondrion that catalyzes the formation of ATP from ADP and inorganic phosphate using the energy supplied by the electron transport chain.

ATPase   Any enzyme that catalyzes a biochemical reaction by extracting the necessary energy from ATP.

autogeneic transplant   A patient receives a transplant of his or her own tissue.

autologous   Refers to tissues or cells derived from the patient's own body.

autosome   Any chromosome other than a sex chromosome.

autoradiograph (autoradiogram)   X-ray film that has been exposed to x-rays or to a source of radioactivity. Used to vissualize internal structures of the body and radioactive signals from sequencing gels and DNA or RNA blots.

axon   A long extension of a neuron's cell body that transmits an electrical signal to other neurons.

axonal transport   The transport of organelles, such as Golgi vesicles, along an axon to the axonal terminus. Transport also flows from the terminus to the cell body.

B cell (B lymphocyte)   A white blood cell that makes antibodies and is part of the adaptive immune response.

bacteria   One of the most ancient forms of cellular life (the other is the archaea). Bacteria are procaryotes and some are known to cause disease.

bacterial artificial chromosome (BAC)   A cloning vector that accommodates DNA inserts of up to 1 million base pairs.

bacteriophage   A virus that infects bacteria. Bacteriophages were used to prove that DNA is the cell's genetic material and are now used as cloning vectors.

base   A substance that can accept a proton in solution. The purines and pyrimidines in DNA and RNA are organic bases and are often referred to simply as bases.

base pair   Two nucleotides in RNA or DNA that are held together by hydrogen bonds. Adenine bound to thymine or guanine bound to cytosine are examples of base pairs

benign   Tumors that grow to a limited size, and do not spread to other parts of the body.

beta sheet   Common structural motif in proteins in which different strands of the protein run alongside each other and are held together by hydrogen bonds.

biopsy   The removal of cells or tissues for examination under a microscope. When only a sample of tissue is removed, the procedure is called an incisional biopsy or core biopsy. When an entire lump or suspicious area is removed, the procedure is called an excisional biopsy. When a sample of tissue or fluid is removed with a needle, the procedure is called a needle biopsy or fine-needle aspiration.

biosphere   The world of living organisms

biotechnology   A set of procedures that are used to study and manipulate genes and their products.

blastomere   A cell formed by the cleavage of a fertilized egg. Blastomeres are the totipotent cells of the early embryo.

blotting   A technique for transferring DNA (Southern blotting), RNA (northern blotting), or proteins (western blotting) from an agarose or polyacrylamide gel to a nylon membrane.

BRCA1 (breast cancer gene 1)   A gene on chromosome 17 that may be involved in regulating the cell cycle. A person who inherits an altered version of the BRCA1 gene has a higher risk of getting breast, ovarian, or prostate cancer.

BRCA2 (breast cancer gene 2)   A gene on chromosome 13 that, when mutated, increases the risk of getting breast, ovarian, or prostate cancer.

budding yeast   The common name for the baker's yeast *Saccharomyces cerevisiae*, a popular experimental organism that reproduces by budding off a parental cell.

buffer   A pH-regulated solution with a known electrolyte (salt) content. Used in the isolation, manipulation, and storage of biomolecules and medicinal products.

cadherin   Belongs to a family of proteins that mediates cell-cell adhesion in animal tissues.

calorie   A unit of heat. One calorie is the amount of heat needed to raise the temperature of 1 gram of water by 1°C. Kilocalories (1000 calories) are used to describe the energy content of foods.

capsid   The protein coat of a virus, formed by autoassembly of one or more proteins into a geometrically symmetrical structure.

carbohydrate   A general class of compounds that includes sugars, containing carbon, hydrogen, and oxygen.

carboxyl group   A carbon atom attached to an oxygen and a hydroxyl group.

carboxyl terminus   The end of a protein containing a carboxyl group.

carcinogen   A compound or form of radiation that can cause cancer.

carcinogenesis   The formation of a cancer.

carcinoma   Cancer of the epithelium, representing the majority of human cancers.

cardiac muscle   Muscle of the heart. Composed of myocytes that are linked together in a communication network based on free passage of small molecules through gap junctions.

caspase   A protease involved in the initiation of apoptosis.

catabolism   Enzyme regulated breakdown of large molecules for the extraction of chemical-bond energy. Intermediate products are called catabolites.

catalyst   A substance that lowers the activation energy of a reaction.

CD28   Cell-surface protein located in T cell membranes, necessary for the activation of T cells by foreign antigens.

cDNA (complementary DNA)   DNA that is synthesized from mRNA, thus containing the complementary sequence. cDNA contains coding sequence, but not the regulatory sequences that are present in the genome. Labeled probes are made from cDNA for the study of gene expression.

cell adhesion molecule (CAM)   A cell surface protein that is used to connect cells to each other.

cell body   The main part of a cell containing the nucleus, Golgi complex, and endoplasmic reticulum. Used in reference to neurons that have long processes (dendrites and axons) extending some distance from the nucleus and cytoplasmic machinery.

cell coat   (see **glycocalyx**)

cell fate   The final differentiated state that a pluripotent embryonic cell is expected to attain.

cell-cycle control system   A team of regulatory proteins that governs progression through the cell cycle.

cell-division-cycle gene (*cdc* gene)   A gene that controls a specific step in the cell cycle.

cell-medicated immune response   Activation of specific cells to launch an immune response against an invading microbe.

cell nuclear transfer   Animal cloning technique whereby a somatic cell nucleus is transferred to an enucleated oocyte. Synonymous with somatic cell nuclear transfer.

celsius   A measure of temperature. This scale is defined such that 0°C is the temperature at which water freezes, and 100°C is the temperature at which water boils.

central nervous system (CNS)   That part of a nervous system that analyzes signals from the body and the environment. In animals, the CNS includes the brain and spinal cord.

centriole   A cylindrical array of microtubules that is found at the center of a centrosome in animal cells.

centromere   A region of a mitotic chromosome that holds sister chromatids together. Microtubules of the spindle fiber connect to an area of the centromere called the kinetochore.

centrosome   Organizes the mitotic spindle and the spindle poles. In most animal cells it contains a pair of centrioles.

chiasma (plural chiasmata)   An X-shaped connection between homologous chromosomes that occurs during meiosis I, representing a site of crossing-over, or genetic exchange between the two chromosomes.

chromatid   A duplicate chromosome that is still connected to the original at the centromere. The identical pair are called sister chromatids.

chromatin   A complex of DNA and proteins (histones and nonhistones) that forms each chromosome, and is found in the nucleus of all eucaryotes. Decondensed and thread-like during interphase.

chromatin condensation   Compaction of different regions of interphase chromosomes that is mediated by the histones.

chromosome   One long molecule of DNA that contains the organism's genes. In procaryotes the chromosome is circular and naked; in eucaryotes it is linear and complexed with histone and nonhistone proteins.

chromosome condensation   Compaction of entire chromosomes in preparation for cell division.

clinical breast exam   An exam of the breast performed by a physician to check for lumps or other changes.

cnidoblast   A stinging cell found in the Cnidarians (jellyfish).

cyclic adenosine monophosphate (cAMP)   A second messenger in a cell-signaling pathway that is produced from ATP by the enzyme adenylate cyclase.

cyclin   A protein that activates protein kinases (cyclin-dependent protein kinases, or Cdk) that control progression from one stage of the cell cycle to another.

cytochemistry   The study of the intracellular distribution of chemicals.

cytochrome   Colored, iron-containing protein that is part of the electron transport chain.

cytotoxic T-cell   A T-lymphocyte that kills infected body cells.

dendrite   An extension of a nerve cell that receives signals from other neurons.

dexrazoxane   A drug used to protect the heart from the toxic effects of anthracycline drugs such as doxorubicin. It belongs to the family of drugs called chemoprotective agents.

dideoxynucleotide   A nucleotide lacking the $2'$ and $3'$ hydroxyl groups.

dideoxy sequencing   A method for sequencing DNA that employs dideoxyribose nucleotides. Also known as the Sanger sequencing method, after Fred Sanger, a chemist who invented the procedure in 1976.

diploid   A genetic term meaning two sets of homologous chromosomes, one set from the mother and the other from the father. Thus, diploid organisms have two versions (alleles) of each gene in the genome.

DNA (deoxyribonucleic acid)   A long polymer formed by linking four different kinds of nucleotides together likes beads on a string. The sequence of nucleotides is used to encode an organism's genes.

DNA helicase   An enzyme that separates and unwinds the two DNA strands in preparation for replication or transcription.

DNA library   A collection of DNA fragments that are cloned into plasmids or viral genomes.

DNA ligase   An enzyme that joins two DNA strands together to make a continuous DNA molecule.

DNA microarray   A technique for studying the simultaneous expression of a very large number of genes.

DNA polymerase   An enzyme that synthesizes DNA using one strand as a template.

DNA primase   An enzyme that synthesizes a short strand of RNA that serves as a primer for DNA replication.

dorsal   The backside of an animal. Also refers to the upper surface of anatomical structures, such as arms or wings.

dorsalventral   The body axis running from the backside to the frontside or the upperside to the underside of a structure.

double helix   The three-dimensional structure of DNA in which the two strands twist around each other to form a spiral.

doxorubicin   An anticancer drug that belongs to a family of antitumor antibiotics.

Drosophila melanogaster   Small species of fly, commonly called a fruit fly that is used as an experimental organism in genetics, embryology, and gerontology.

ductal carcinoma in situ (DCIS)   Abnormal cells that involve only the lining of a breast duct. The cells have not spread outside the duct to other tissues in the breast. Also called intraductal carcinoma.

dynein   A motor protein that is involved in chromosome movements during cell division.

dysplasia   Disordered growth of cells in a tissue or organ, often leading to the development of cancer.

ectoderm   An embryonic tissue that is the precursor of the epidermis and the nervous system.

electrochemical gradient   A differential concentration of an ion or molecule across the cell membrane that serves as a source of potential energy and may polarize the cell electrically.

electron microscope   A microscope that uses electrons to produce a high resolution image of the cell.

electrophoresis   The movement of a molecule, such as protein, DNA or RNA, through an electric field. In practice, the molecules migrate through a slab of agarose or polyacrylamide that is immersed in a special solution and subjected to an electric field.

elution   To remove one substance from another by washing it out with a buffer or solvent.

embryogenesis   The development of an embryo from a fertilized egg.

embryonic stem cell (ES cell)   A pluripotent cell derived from the inner cell mass (the cells that give rise to the embryo instead of the placenta) of a mammalian embryo.

endocrine cell   A cell that is specialized for the production and release of hormones. Such cells make up hormone-producing tissue such as the pituitary gland or gonads.

endocytosis   Cellular uptake of material from the environment by invagination of the cell membrane to form a vesicle called an endosome. The endosome's contents are made available to the cell after it fuses with a lysosome.

endoderm   An embryonic tissue layer that gives rise to the gut.

endoplasmic reticulum (ER)   Membrane-bounded chambers that are used to modify newly synthesized proteins with the addition of sugar molecules (glycosylation). When finished, the glycosylated proteins are sent to the Golgi apparatus in exocytotic vesicles.

enhancer   A DNA regulatory sequence that provides a binding site for transcription factors capable of increasing the rate of transcription for a specific gene. Often located thousands of base pairs away from the gene it regulates.

enveloped virus   A virus, containing a capsid that is surrounded by a lipid bilayer originally obtained from the membrane of a previously infected cell.

enzyme   A protein or RNA that catalyzes a specific chemical reaction.

epidermis   The epithelial layer, or skin, that covers the outer surface of the body.

ER marker sequence   The amino terminal sequence that directs proteins to enter the endoplasmic reticulum (ER). This sequence is removed once the protein enters the ER.

erythrocyte   A red blood cell that contains the oxygen-carrying pigment hemoglobin, used to deliver oxygen to cells in the body.

***Escherichia coli* (*E. coli*)**   Rod shape, gram negative, bacterium that inhabits the intestinal tract of most animals and is used as an experimental organism by geneticists and biomedical researchers.

eukaryote (eucaryote)   A cell containing a nucleus and many membrane-bounded organelles. All lifeforms, except bacteria and viruses, are composed of eucaryote cells.

euchromatin   Lightly staining portion of interphase chromatin, in contrast to the darkly staining heterochromatin (condensed chromatin). Euchromatin contains most, if not all, of the active genes.

exocytosis   The process by which molecules are secreted from a cell. Molecules to be secreted are located in Golgi-derived vesicles that fuse with the inner surface of the cell membrane, depositing the contents into the intercellular space.

exon   Coding region of a eucaryote gene that is represented in messenger RNA, and thus directs the synthesis of a specific protein.

expression studies   Examination of the type and quantity of mRNA or protein that is produced by cells, tissues, or organs.

fat   A lipid material, consisting of triglycerides (fatty acids bound to glycerol), that is stored adipocytes as an energy reserve.

fatty acid   A compound that has a carboxylic acid attached to a long hydrocarbon chain. A major source of cellular energy and a component of phospholipids.

fertilization   The fusion of haploid male and female gametes to form a diploid zygote.

fibroblast   The cell type that, by secreting an extracellular matrix, gives rise to the connective tissue of the body.

Filopodium   A finger-like projection of a cell's cytoplasmic membrane, commonly observed in amoeba and embryonic nerve cells.

filter hybridization   The detection of specific DNA or RNA molecules, fixed on a nylon filter (or membrane), by incubating the filter with a labelled probe that hybridizes to the target sequence. Also known as membrane hybridization.

fixative   A chemical that is used to preserve cells and tissues. Common examples are formaldehyde, methanol, and acetic acid.

flagellum (plural flagella)   Whip-like structure found in procaryotes and eucaryotes that are used to propel cells through water.

fluorescein   Fluorescent dye that produces a green light when illuminated with ultraviolet or blue light.

fluorescent dye A dye that absorbs UV or blue light, and emits light of a longer wavelength, usually as green or red light.

fluorescent in situ hybridization (FISH) A procedure for detecting the expression of a specific gene in tissue sections or smears through the use of DNA probes labelled with a fluorescent dye.

fluorescent microscope A microscope that is equipped with special filters, and a beam splitter, for the examination of tissues and cells stained with a fluorescent dye.

follicle cell Cells that surround, and help feed, a developing oocyte.

G_0 G "zero" refers to a phase of the cell cycle. State of withdrawal from the cycle as the cell enters a resting or quiescent stage. Occurs in differentiated body cells, as well as developing oocytes.

G_1 Gap 1 refers to the phase of the cell cycle that occurs just after mitosis, and before the next round of DNA synthesis.

G_2 The Gap 2 phase of the cell cycle follows DNA replication and precedes mitosis.

gap junction A communication channel in the membranes of adjacent cells that allows free passage of ions and small molecules.

gel electrophoresis A procedure that is used to separate biomolecules by forcing them to migrate through a gel matrix (agarose or polyacrylamide) subjected to an electric field.

gene A region of the DNA that specifies a specific protein or RNA molecule that is handed down from one generation to the next. This region includes both the coding, noncoding and regulatory sequences.

gene regulatory protein Any protein that binds to DNA and thereby affects the expression of a specific gene.

gene repressor protein A protein that binds to DNA and blocks transcription of a specific gene.

gene therapy A method for treating disease whereby a defective gene, causing the disease, is either repaired, replaced or supplemented with a functional copy.

genetic code A set of rules that assigns a specific DNA or RNA triplet, consisting of a three base sequence, to a specific amino acid.

genome All of the genes that belong to a cell or an organism.

genomic library A collection of DNA fragments, obtained by digesting genomic DNA with a restriction enzyme, that are cloned into plasmid or viral vectors.

genomics   The study of DNA sequences and their role in the function and structure of an organism.

genotype   The genetic composition of a cell or organism.

germ cell   Cells that develop into gametes, either sperm or oocytes.

glucose   Six-carbon monoosaccharide (sugar) that is the principle source of energy for many cells and organisms. Stored as glycogen in animal cells and as starch in plants. Wood is an elaborate polymer of glucose and other sugars.

glycerol   A three carbon alcohol that is an important component of phospholipids.

glycocalyx   A molecular "forest", consisting of glycosylated proteins and lipids, that covers the surface of every cell. The glycoproteins and glycolipids, carried to the cell membrane by Golgi-derived vesicles, have many functions including the formation of ion channels, cell-signaling receptors, and transporters.

glycogen   A polymer of glucose, used to store energy in an animal cell.

glycolysis   The degradation of glucose with production of ATP.

glycoprotein   Any protein that has a chain of glucose molecules (oligosaccharide) attached to some of the amino acid residues.

glycosylation   The process of adding one or more sugar molecules to proteins or lipids.

glycosyl transferase   An enzyme in the Golgi complex that adds glucose to proteins.

Golgi complex (Golgi apparatus)   Membrane-bounded organelle in eucaryote cells that receives glycoproteins from the ER, which are modified and sorted before being sent to their final destination. The Golgi complex is also the source of glycolipids that are destined for the cell membrane. The glycoproteins and glycolipids leave the Golgi by exocytosis. This organelle is named after the Italian histologist, Camillo Golgi, who discovered it in 1898.

Gram stain   A bacterial stain that detects different species of bacteria based on the composition of their cell wall. Bacteria that retain the Gram stain are colored blue (Gram positive), whereas those that do not are colored orange (Gram negative).

granulocyte   A type of white blood cell that includes the neutrophils, basophils, and eosinophils.

growth factor   A small protein (polypeptide) that can stimulate cells to grow and proliferate.

haploid   Having only one set of chromosomes. A condition that is typical in gametes, such as sperm and eggs.

HeLa cell   A tumor-derived cell line, originally isolated from a cancer patient in 1951. Currently used by many laboratories to study the cell biology of cancer and carcinogenesis.

helix-loop-helix   A structural motif common to a group of gene regulatory proteins.

helper T cell   A type of T lymphocyte that helps stimulate B cells to make antibody directed against a specific microbe or antigen.

hemoglobin   An iron-containing protein complex, located in red blood cell, that picks up oxygen in the lungs and carries it to other tissues and cells of the body.

hemopoiesis   Production of blood cells, occurring primarily in the bone marrow.

hematopoietic   Refers to cells, derived form the bone marrow, that give rise to red and white blood cells.

hematopoietic stem cell transplantation (HSCT)   The use of stem cells isolated from the bone marrow to treat leukemia and lymphoma.

hepatocyte   A liver cell.

heterochromatin   A region of a chromosome that is highly condensed and transcriptionally inactive.

histochemistry   The study of chemical differentiation of tissues.

histology   The study of tissues.

histone   Small nuclear proteins, rich in the amino acids arginine and lysine, that form the nucleosome in eucaryote nuclei, a bead-like structure that is a major component of chromatin.

HIV   The human immunodeficiency virus that is responsible for AIDS.

homolog   One of two or more genes that have a similar sequence, and are descended from a common ancestor gene.

homologous   Organs or molecules that are similar in structure because they have descended from a common ancestor. Used primarily in reference to DNA and protein sequences.

homologous chromosomes   Two copies of the same chromosome, one inherited from the mother, and the other from the father.

hormone   A signaling molecule, produced and secreted by endocrine glands. Usually released into general circulation for coordination of an animal's physiology.

housekeeping gene   A gene that codes for a protein that is needed by all cells, irregardless of the cell's specialization. Genes encoding enzymes involved in glycolysis and Krebs cycle are common examples.

hybridization   A term used in molecular biology (recombinant DNA technology), meaning the formation a double stranded nucleic acid through complementary base-pairing. A property that is exploited in filter hybridization, a procedure that is used to screen gene libraries, and to study gene structure and expression.

hydrolysis   The breaking of a covalent chemical bond with the subsequent addition of a molecule of water.

hydrophilic   A polar compound that mixes readily with water.

hydrophobic   A non-polar molecule that dissolves in fat and lipid solutions, but not in water.

hydroxyl group (-OH)   Chemical group consisting of oxygen and hydrogen that is a prominent part of alcohol.

image analysis   A computerized method for extracting information from digitized microscopic images of cells or cell organelles.

immunofluorescence   Detection of specific a cellular protein with the aid of a fluorescent dye that is coupled to an antibody.

immunoglobulin (Ig)   An antibody made by B cells as part of the adaptive immune response.

incontinence   Inability to control the flow of urine from the bladder (urinary incontinence) or the escape of stool from the rectum (fecal incontinence).

insertional mutagenesis   Damage suffered by a gene when a virus or a jumping gene inserts itself into a chromosome.

in situ **hybridization**   A method for studying gene expression, whereby a labeled cDNA or RNA probe hybridizes to a specific mRNA in intact cells or tissues. The procedure is usually carried out on tissue sections or smears of individual cells.

in vitro   Refers to cells growing in culture, or a biochemical reaction occurring in a test tube (Latin for "in glass").

in vivo   A biochemical reaction, or a process, occurring in living cells or a living organism (Latin for "in life").

insulin Polypeptide hormone secreted by β (beta) cells in the vertebrate pancreas. Production of this hormone is regulated directly by the amount of glucose that is in the blood.

interleukin A small protein hormone, secreted by lymphocytes, to activate and coordinate the adaptive immune response.

interphase The period between each cell division, which includes the G_1, S, and G_2 phases of the cell cycle.

intron A section of a eucaryotic gene that is non-coding. It is transcribed, but does not appear in the mature mRNA.

ion channel A transmembrane channel that allows ions to diffuse across the membrane, down their electrochemical gradient.

ion An atom that has gained or lossed electrons, thus acquiring a charge. Common examples are Na^+ and Ca^{++} ions.

ischemia An inadequate supply of blood to a part of the body, caused by degenerative vascular disease.

Jak-STAT signaling pathway One of several cell signaling pathways that activates gene expression. The pathway is activated through cell surface receptors and cytoplasmic Janus kinases (Jaks), and signal transducers and activators of transcription (STATs).

karyotype A pictorial catalog of a cell's chromosomes, showing their number, size, shape, and overall banding pattern.

keratin Proteins produced by specialized epithelial cells called keratinocytes. Keratin is found in hair, fingernails, and feathers.

kilometer 1,000 meters, which is equal to 0.621 miles.

kinesin A motor protein that uses energy obtained from the hydrolysis of ATP to move along a microtubule.

kinetochore A complex of proteins that forms around the centromere of mitotic or meiotic chromosomes, providing an attachment site for microtubules. The other end of each microtubule is attached to a chromosome.

Krebs cycle (citric acid cycle) The central metabolic pathway in all eucaryotes and aerobic procaryotes. Discovered by the German chemist, Hans Krebs, in 1937. The cycle oxidizes acetyl groups derived from food molecules. The end products are CO_2, H_2O, and high-energy electrons, which pass via NADH and FADH2 to the respiratory chain. In eucaryotes, Krebs cycle is located in the mitochondria.

labeling reaction   The addition of a radioactive atom or fluorescent dye to DNA or RNA for use as a probe in filter hybridization.

lagging strand   One of the two newly synthesized DNA strands at a replication fork. The lagging strand is synthesized discontinuously, and therefore, its completion lags behind the second, or leading, strand.

lambda bacteriophage   A viral parasite that infects bacteria. Widely used as a DNA cloning vector.

leading strand   One of the two newly synthesized DNA strands at a replication fork. The leading strand is made by continuous synthesis in the 5′ to 3′ direction.

leucine zipper   A structural motif of DNA binding proteins, in which two identical proteins are joined together at regularly-spaced leucine residues, much like a zipper, to form a dimer.

leukemia   Cancer of white blood cells

lipid bilayer   Two, closely aligned, sheets of phospholipids that forms the core structure of all cell membranes. The two layers are aligned such that the hydrophobic tails are interior, while the hydrophilic head groups are exterior on both surfaces.

liposome   An artificial lipid bilayer vesicle used in membrane studies and as an artificial gene therapy vector.

locus   A term from genetics that refers to the position of a gene along a chromosome. Different alleles of the same gene occupy the same locus.

long-term potentiation (LTP)   A physical remodeling of synaptic junctions that receive continuous stimulation.

Lumen   A cavity completely surrounded by epithelial cells.

lymphocyte   A type of white blood cell that is involved in the adaptive immune response. There are two kinds of lymphocytes: T lymphocytes and B lymphocytes. T lymphocytes (T cells) mature in the thymus, and attack invading microbes directly. B lymphocytes (B cells) mature in the bone marrow, and make antibodies that are designed to immobilize or destroy specific microbes or antigens.

lysis   The rupture of the cell membrane followed by death of the cell.

lysosome   Membrane -bounded organelle of eucaryotes that contains powerful digestive enzymes.

macromolecule   A very large molecule that is built from smaller molecular subunits. Common examples are DNA, proteins, and polysaccharides.

magnetic resonance imaging (MRI)   A procedure in which radio waves and a powerful magnet linked to a computer are used to create detailed pictures of areas inside the body. These pictures can show the difference between normal and diseased tissue. MRI makes better images of organs and soft tissue than other scanning techniques, such as CT or x-ray. MRI is especially useful for imaging the brain, spine, the soft tissue of joints, and the inside of bones. Also called nuclear magnetic resonance imaging.

major histocompatibility complex   Vertebrate genes that code for a large family of cell-surface glycoproteins that bind foreign antigens and present them to T cells to induce an immune response.

malignant   Refers to the functional status of a cancer cell that grows aggressively and is able to metastasize, or colonize, other areas of the body.

mammography   The use of x-rays to create a picture of the breast.

MAP-kinase (mitogen-activated protein kinase)   A protein kinase that is part of a cell proliferation-inducing signaling pathway.

M-cyclin   A eucaryote enzyme that regulates mitosis.

meiosis   A special form of cell division by which haploid gametes are produced. This is accomplished with two rounds of cell division, but only one round of DNA replication.

melanocyte   A skin cell that produces the pigment melanin.

membrane   The lipid bilayer, and the associated glycocalyx, that surrounds and encloses all cells.

membrane channel   A protein complex that forms a pore or channel through the membrane for the free passage of ions and small molecules.

membrane potential   A build-up of charged ions on one side of the cell membrane establishes an electrochemical gradient that is measured in millivolts (mV). An important characteristic of neurons as it provides the electrical current, when ion channels open, that enable these cells to communicate with each other.

mesoderm   An embryonic germ layer that gives rise to muscle, connective tissue, bones, and many internal organs.

messenger RNA (mRNA) An RNA transcribed from a gene that is used as the gene template by the ribosomes, and other components of the translation machinery, to synthesize a protein.

metabolism The sum total of the chemical processes that occur in living cells.

metaphase The stage of mitosis at which the chromosomes are attached to the spindle but have not begun to move apart.

metaphase plate Refers to the imaginary plane established by the chromosomes as they line up at right angles to the spindle poles.

metaplasia A change in the pattern of cellular behavior that often precedes the development of cancer.

metastasis Spread of cancer cells from the site of the original tumor to other parts of the body.

methyl group (-CH₃) Hydrophobic chemical group derived from methane. Occurs at the end of a fatty acid.

meter Basic unit in the metric system. Equal to 39.4 inches or 1.09 yards.

micrograph Photograph taken through a light, or electron, microscope.

micrometer (μm or micron) Equal to 10^{-6} meters.

microtubule A fine cylindrical tube made of the protein tubulin, forming a major component of the eucaryote cytoskeleton.

millimeter (mm) Equal to 10^{-3} meters.

mitochondrion (plural mitochondria) Eucaryote organelle, formerly free-living, that produces most of the cell's ATP

mitogen A hormone or signaling molecule that stimulates cells to grow and divide.

mitosis Division of a eucaryotic nucleus. From the Greek *mitos,* meaning a thread, in reference to the threadlike appearance of interphase chromosomes.

mitotic chromosome Highly condensed duplicated chromosomes held together by the centromere. Each member of the pair is referred to as a sister chromatid.

mitotic spindle Array of microtubules, fanning out from the polar centrioles, and connecting to each of the chromosomes.

molecule Two or more atoms linked together by covalent bonds.

monoclonal Antibody   An antibody produced from a B-cell derived clonal line. Since all of the cells are clones of the original B cell, the antibodies produced are identical.

monocyte   A type of white blood cell that is involved in the immune response.

motif   An element of structure or pattern that and may be a recurring domain in a variety of proteins.

M phase   The period of the cell cycle (mitosis or meiosis) when the chromosomes separate and migrate to the opposite poles of the spindle.

multipass transmembrane protein   A membrane protein that passes back and forth across the lipid bilayer.

multipotency   The property by which an undifferentiated animal cell can give rise to many of the body's cell types.

mutant   A genetic variation within a population.

mutation   A heritable change in the nucleotide sequence of a chromosome.

myelin sheath   Insulation applied to the axons of neurons. The sheath is produced by oligodendrocytes in the central nervous system, and by Schwann cells in the peripheral nervous system.

myeloid cell   White blood cells other than lymphocytes.

myoblast   Muscle precursor cell. Many myoblasts fuse into a syncytium, containing many nuclei, to form a single muscle cell.

myocyte   A muscle cell.

NAD (nicotine adenine dinucleotide)   Accepts a hydride ion (H^-), produced by the Krebs cycle, forming NADH, the main carrier of electrons for oxidative phosphorylation.

NADH dehydrogenase   Removes electrons from NADH and passes them down the electron transport chain.

nanometer (nm)   Equal to 10^{-9} meters or 10^{-3} microns.

National Institutes of Health (NIH)   A biomedical research center located in the United States. NIH consists of over 25 research institutes, including the National Institute of Aging (NIA) and the National Cancer Institute (NCI). All of the institutes are funded by the federal government.

natural killer cell (NK cell)   A lymphocyte that kills virus-infected cells in the body. They also kill foreign cells associated with a tissue or organ transplant.

neuromuscular junction   A special form of synapse between a motor neuron and a skeletal muscle cell.

neuron   A cell specially adapted for communication that forms the nervous system of all animals.

neuromodulator   A chemical released by neurons at a synapse that modifies the behavior of the targeted neuron(s).

neurotransmitter   A chemical released by neurons at a synapse that activates the targeted neuron.

non-small cell lung cancer   A group of lung cancers that includes squamous cell carcinoma, adenocarcinoma, and large cell carcinoma. The small cells are endocrine cells.

northern blotting   A technique for the study of gene expression. Messenger RNA (mRNA) is fractionated on an agarose gel and then transferred to a piece of nylon filter paper (or membrane). A specific mRNA is detected by hybridization with a labeled DNA or RNA probe. The original blotting technique invented by E. M. Southern inspired the name. Also known as RNA blotting.

nuclear envelope   The double membrane (two lipid bilayers) enclosing the cell nucleus.

nuclear localization signal (NLS)   A short amino acid sequence located on proteins that are destined for the cell nucleus, after they are translated in the cytoplasm.

nuclei acid   DNA or RNA, a macromolecule consisting of a chain of nucleotides.

nucleolar organizer   Region of a chromosome containing a cluster of ribosomal RNA genes that gives rise to the nucleolus.

nucleolus   A structure in the nucleus where ribosomal RNA is transcribed and ribosomal subunits are assembled.

nucleoside   A purine or pyrimidine linked to a ribose or deoxyribose sugar.

nucleosome   A bead-like structure, consisting of histone proteins.

nucleotide   A nucleoside containing one or more phosphate groups linked to the 5' carbon of the ribose sugar. DNA and RNA are nucleotide polymers.

nucleus   Eucaryote cell organelle that contains the DNA genome on one or more chromosomes.

oligodendrocyte   A myelinating glia cell of the vertebrate central nervous system.

oligomer   A short polymer, usually consisting of amino acids (oligopeptides), sugars (oligosaccharides), or nucleotides (oligonucleotides). Taken from the Greek word, *oligos,* meaning few or little.

oligo labeling   A method for incorporating labeled nucleotides into a short piece of DNA or RNA. Also known as the random-primer labeling method.

oncogene   A mutant form of a normal cellular gene, known as a proto-oncogene, that can transform a cell to a cancerous phenotype.

oocyte   A female gamete or egg cell.

operator   A region of a procaryote chromosome that controls the expression of adjacent genes.

operon   Two or more procaryote genes that are transcribed into a single mRNA.

organelle   A membrane bounded structure, occurring in eucaryote cells, that has a specialized function. Examples are the nucleus, Golgi complex and endoplasmic reticulum.

osmosis   The movement of solvent across a semi-permeable membrane that separates a solution with a high concentration of solutes from one with a low concentration of solutes. The membrane must be permeable to the solvent, but not to the solutes. In the context of cellular osmosis, the solvent is always water, the solutes are ions and molecules, and the membrane is the cell membrane.

osteoblast   Cells that form bones.

ovulation   Rupture of a mature follicle with subsequent release of a mature oocyte from the ovary.

oxidative phosphorylation   Generation of high energy electrons from food molecules that are used to power the synthesis of ATP from ADP and inorganic phosphate. The electrons are eventually transferred to oxygen, to complete the process. Occurs in bacteria and mitochondria.

p53 A tumor suppressor gene that is mutated in about half of all human cancers. The normal function of the *p53* protein is to block passage through the cell cycle when DNA damage is detected.

parthenogenesis A natural form of animal cloning whereby an individual is produced without the formation of haploid gametes and the fertilization of an egg.

pathogen An organism that causes disease.

PCR (polymerase chain reaction) A method for amplifying specific regions of DNA by temperature cycling a reaction mixture containing the template, a heat-stable DNA polymerase, and replication primers.

peptide bond The chemical bond that links amino acids together to form a protein.

pH Measures the acidity of a solution as a negative logarithmic function (p) of H^+ concentration (H). Thus, a pH of 2.0 (10^{-2} molar H^+) is acidic, whereas a pH of 8.0 (10^{-8} molar H^+) is basic.

phagocyte A cell that engulfs other cells or debri by phagocytosis.

phagocytosis A process whereby cells engulf other cells or organic material by endocytosis. A common practice among protozoans, and cells of the vertebrate immune system. (From the Greek *phagein,* to eat)

phenotype Physical characteristics of a cell or organism.

phospholipid The kind of lipid molecule used to construct cell membranes. Composed of a hydrophilic head-group, phosphate, glycerol, and two hydrophobic fatty acid tails.

phosphorylation A chemical reaction in which a phosphate is covalently bonded to another molecule.

phosphokinase An enzyme that adds phosphate to proteins.

photoreceptor A molecule or cell that responds to light.

photosynthesis A biochemical process in which plants, algae, and certain bacteria use energy obtained from sunlight to synthesize macromolecules from CO_2 and H_2O.

phylogeny The evolutionary history of a group of organisms, usually represented diagrammatically as a phylogenetic tree.

pinocytosis A form of endocytosis whereby fluid is brought into the cell from the environment.

pixel   One element in a data array that represents an image or photograph.

placebo   An inactive substance that looks the same, and is administered in the same way, as a drug in a clinical trial.

plasmid   A minichromosome, often carrying antibiotic-resistant genes, that occurs naturally among procaryotes. Used extensively as a DNA cloning vector.

platelet   A cell fragment, derived from megakaryocytes and lacking a nucleus, that is present in the bloodstream, and is involved in blood coagulation.

ploidy   The total number of chromosomes (n) that a cell has. Ploidy is also measured as the amount of DNA (C) in a given cell, relative to a haploid nucleus of the same organism. Most organisms are diploid, having two sets of chromosomes, one from each parent, but there is great variation among plants and animals. The silk gland of the moth *Bombyx mori,* for example, has cells that are extremely polyploid, reaching values of 100,000C, flowers are often highly polyploid, and vertebrate hepatocytes may be 16C.

pluripotency   The property by which an undifferentiated animal cell can give rise to most of the body's cell types.

poikilotherm   An animal incapable of regulating its body temperature independent of the external environment. It is for this reason that such animals are restricted to warm tropical climates.

point mutation   A change in DNA, particularly in a region containing a gene, that alters a single nucleotide.

Polarization   A term used to describe the re-establishment of a sodium ion gradient across the membrane of a neuron. Polarization followed by depolarization is the fundamental mechanism by which neurons communicate with each other.

polyploid   Possessing more than two sets of homologous chromosomes.

polyploidization   DNA replication in the absence of cell division. Provides many copies of particular genes and thus occurs in cells that highly active metabolically (see ploidy).

polyacrylamide   A tough polymer gel that is used to fractionate DNA and protein samples.

portal system A system of liver vessels that carries liver enzymes directly to the digestive tract.

post-mitotic Refers to a cell that has lost the ability to divide.

probe Usually a fragment of a cloned DNA molecule that is labeled with a radioisotope or fluorescent dye, and used to detect specific DNA or RNA molecules on Southern or Northern blots.

progenitor cell A cell that has developed from a stem cell, but can still give rise to a limited variety of cell types.

proliferation A process whereby cells grow and divide.

promoter A DNA sequence to which RNA polymerase binds to initiate gene transcription.

prophase The first stage of mitosis. The chromosomes are duplicated and are beginning to condense, but are attached to the spindle.

protein A major constituent of cells and organisms. Proteins, made by linking amino acids together, are used for structural purposes, and regulate many biochemical reactions in their alternative role as enzymes. Proteins range in size from just a few amino acids to over 200.

protein glycosylation The addition of sugar molecules to a protein.

proto-oncogene A normal gene that can be converted to a cancer-causing gene (oncogene) by a point mutation or through inappropriate expression.

protozoa Free living, single-cell eucaryotes that feed on bacteria and other microorganisms. Common examples are *Paramecium* and *Amoeba*. Parasitic forms are also known that inhabit the digestive and urogenital tract of many animals, including humans.

P-site The binding site on the ribosome for the growing protein (or peptide) chain.

purine A nitrogen-containing compound that is found in RNA and DNA. Two examples are adenine and guanine.

pyrimidine A nitrogen-containing compound found in RNA and DNA. Examples are cytosine, thymine and uracil (RNA only).

radioactive isotope An atom with an unstable nucleus that emits radiation as it decays.

random primer labeling A method for incorporating labeled nucleotides into a short piece of DNA or RNA.

randomized clinical trial   A study in which the participants are assigned by chance to separate groups that compare different treatments; neither the researchers nor the participants can choose which group. Using chance to assign people to groups means that the groups will be similar and that the treatments they receive can be compared objectively. At the time of the trial, it is not known which treatment is best.

reagent   A chemical solution designed for a specific biochemical or histochemical procedure.

recombinant DNA   A DNA molecule that has been formed by joining two or more fragments from different sources.

refractive index   A measure of the ability of a substance to bend a beam of light expressed in reference to air which has, by definition, a refractive index of 1.0.

regulatory sequence   A DNA sequence to which proteins bind that regulate the assembly of the transcriptional machinery.

replication bubble   Local dissociation of the DNA double helix in preparation for replication. Each bubble contains two replication forks.

replication fork   The Y-shape region of a replicating chromosome. Associated with replication bubbles.

replication origin (origin of replication, ORI)   The location at which DNA replication begins.

respiratory chain (electron transport chain)   A collection of iron- and copper-containing proteins, located in the inner mitochondrion membrane, that utilize the energy of electrons traveling down the chain to synthesize ATP

restriction map   The size and number of DNA fragments obtained after digesting with one or more restriction enzymes.

restriction enzyme   An enzyme that cuts DNA at specific sites.

retrovirus   A virus that converts its RNA genome to DNA once it has infected a cell.

reverse transcriptase   An RNA-dependent DNA polymerase. This enzyme synthesizes DNA by using RNA as a template, the reverse of the usual flow of genetic information from DNA to RNA.

ribosomal RNA (rRNA)   RNA that is part of the ribosome, and serves both a structural and functional role, possibly by catalyzing some of the steps involved in protein synthesis.

ribosome   A complex of protein and RNA that catalyzes the synthesis of proteins.

rough endoplasmic reticulum (rough ER)   Endoplasmic reticulum that has ribosomes bound to its outer surface.

Saccharomyces   Genus of budding yeast that are frequently used in the study of eucaryote cell biology.

sarcoma   Cancer of connective tissue.

Schwann cell   Glia cell that produces myelin in the peripheral nervous system.

screening   Checking for disease when there are no symptoms.

senescence   (from the Latin word *senex*, meaning "old man" or "old age") Physical and biochemical changes that occur in cells and organisms with age.

signal transduction   A process by which a signal is relayed to the interior of a cell where it elicits a response at the cytoplasmic or nuclear level.

smooth muscle cell   Muscles lining the intestinal tract and arteries. Lacks the striations typical of cardiac and skeletal muscle, giving it a smooth appearance when viewed under a microscope.

somatic cell   Any cell in a plant or animal except those that produce gametes (germ cells or germ cell precursors).

somatic cell nuclear transfer   Animal cloning technique whereby a somatic cell nucleus is transferred to an enucleated oocyte. Synonymous with cell nuclear transfer or replacement.

Southern transfer   The transfer of DNA fragments from an agarose gel to a piece of nylon filter paper. Specific fragments are identified by hybridizing the filter to a labeled probe. Invented by the Scottish scientist, E. M. Southern, in 1975. Also known as DNA blotting.

stem cell   Pluripotent progenitor cell, found in embryos and various parts of the body, that can differentiate into a wide variety of cell types.

steroid   A hydrophobic molecule with a characteristic four-ringed structure. Sex hormones, such as estrogen and testosterone, are steroids.

structural gene   A gene that codes for a protein or an RNA. Distinguished from regions of the DNA that are involved in regulating gene expression, but are noncoding.

synapse   A neural communication junction between an axon and a dendrite. Signal transmission occurs when neurotransmitters, released into the junction by the axon of one neuron, stimulate receptors on the dendrite of a second neuron.

syncytium   A large multi-nucleated cell. Skeletal muscle cells are syncytiums produced by the fusion of many myoblasts.

syngeneic transplants   A patient receives tissue or an organ from an identical twin.

tamoxifen   A drug that is used to treat breast cancer. Tamoxifen blocks the effects of the hormone estrogen in the body. It belongs to the family of drugs called antiestrogens.

T cell (T lymphocyte)   A white blood cell involved in activating and coordinating the immune response.

telomere   The end of a chromosome. Replaced by the enzyme telomerase with each round of cell division to prevent shortening of the chromosomes.

telophase   The final stage of mitosis in which the chromosomes decondense and the nuclear envelope reforms.

template   A single strand of DNA or RNA whose sequence serves as a guide for the synthesis of a complementary, or daughter, strand.

therapeutic cloning   The cloning of a human embryo for the purpose of harvesting the inner cell mass (embryonic stem cells).

topoisomerase   An enzyme that makes reversible cuts in DNA to relieve strain or to undo knots.

totipotency   The property by which an undifferentiated animal cell can give rise to all of the body's cell types. The fertilized egg and blastomeres from an early embryo are the only cells possessing this ability.

trans Golgi network   The membrane surfaces where glycoproteins and glycolipids exit the Golgi complex in transport vesicles.

transcription   The copying of a DNA sequence into RNA, catalyzed by RNA polymerase.

transcription factor   A general term referring to a wide assortment of proteins needed to initiate or regulate transcription.

transfection   Introduction of a foreign gene into a eukaryote or prokaryote cell.

transfer RNA (tRNA)   A collection of small RNA molecules that transfer an amino acid to a growing polypeptide chain on a ribosome. There is a separate tRNA for amino acid.

transgenic organism   A plant or animal that has been transfected with a foreign gene.

translation   A ribosome-catalyzed process whereby the nucleotide sequence of a mRNA is used as a template to direct the synthesis of a protein.

transposable element (transposon)   A segment of DNA that can move from one region of a genome to another.

ultrasound (ultrasonography)   A procedure in which high-energy sound waves (ultrasound) are bounced off internal tissues or organs producing echoes that are used to form a picture of body tissues (a sonogram).

umbilical cord blood stem cells   Stem cells, produced by a human fetus and the placenta, that are found in the blood that passes from the placenta to the fetus.

vector   A virus or plasmid used to carry a DNA fragment into a bacterial cell (for cloning) or into a eukaryote to produce a transgenic organism.

vesicle   A membrane-bounded bubble found in eucaryote cells. Vesicles carry material from the ER to the Golgi and from the Golgi to the cell membrane.

virus   A particle containing an RNA or DNA genome surrounded by a protein coat. Viruses are cellular parasites that cause many diseases.

western blotting   The transfer of protein from a polyacrylamide gel too a piece of nylon filter paper. Specific proteins are detected with labeled antibodies. The name was inspired by the original blotting technique invented by the Scottish scientist E. M. Southern in 1975. Also known as protein blotting.

xenogeneic transplants (xenograft)   A patient receives tissue or an organ from an animal of a different species.

yeast   Common term for unicellular eucaryotes that are used to brew beer and make bread. Bakers yeast, *Saccharomyces cerevisiae,* are also widely used in studies on cell biology.

zygote   A diploid cell produced by the fusion of a sperm and egg.

# Further Resources

BOOKS

Alberts, Bruce, Dennis Bray, Karen Hopkins, and Alexander Johnson. *Essential Cell Biology.* Second edition. New York: Garland Publishing, 2003. A basic introduction to cellular structure and function that is suitable for high school students.

Alberts, Bruce, Alexander Johnson, Julian Lewis, Martin Raff, Keith Roberts, and Peter Walter. *Molecular Biology of the Cell.* Fifth edition. New York: Garland Publishing, 2008. Advanced coverage of cell biology that is suitable for senior high school and university students.

Boyles, Peter, and Bernard Levin, editors. *The World Cancer Report 2008.* Lyon, France: The International Agency for Research on Cancer, 2008. Available online. URL: http://www.iarc.fr/. Accessed January 1, 2009. The definitive source for cancer data from around the world.

Brooks, George, Karen Carroll, Janet Butel, and Stephen Morse. *Medical Microbiology, 24th Edition.* New York: McGraw-Hill, 2007. This book devotes an entire section to virology, which includes general properties of viruses, taxonomy, and viral diseases.

Ganong, William. *Review of Medical Physiology.* Twenty-second edition. New York: McGraw-Hill, 2005. A well-written overview of human physiology, beginning with the basic properties of cells and tissues.

Krause, W. J. *Krause's Essential Human Histology for Medical Students.* Boca Raton, Fla.: Universal Publishers, 2005. This book goes well with histology videos provided free on Google video.

Panno, Joseph. *Aging: Modern Theories and Therapies.* Revised edition. New York: Facts On File, 2010. Explains why and how people age and how gene therapy may be used to reverse or modify the process.

———. *Animal Cloning: The Science of Nuclear Transfer.* Revised edition. New York: Facts On File, 2010. Medical applications of cloning technology, including therapeutic cloning, are discussed.

———. *Cancer: The Role of Genes, Lifestyle, and Environment.* Revised edition. New York: Facts On File, 2010. The basic nature of cancer written for the general public and young students.

———. *The Cell: Exploring Nature's First Life-form.* Revised edition. New York: Facts On File, 2010. Everything you need to know about the cell without having to read a 1,000-page textbook.

———. *Stem Cell Research: Medical Applications and Ethical Controversies.* Revised edition. New York: Facts On File, 2010. All about a special type of cell, the stem cell, and its use in medical therapies.

———. *Viruses: The Origin and Evolution of Deadly Pathogens.* New York: Facts On File, 2011. A detailed overview of viral taxonomy, diseases, and pandemics.

JOURNALS AND MAGAZINES

Bainbridge, James, et al. "Effect of Gene Therapy on Visual Function in Leber's Congenital Amaurosis." *The New England Journal of Medicine* 358 (May 22, 2008): 2,231–2,239. A British group, led by Dr. Robin Ali, used gene therapy to restore the night vision in a patient suffering from retinal dystrophy.

Blaese, Michael, et al. "T Lymphocyte-directed Gene Therapy for ADA-SCID: Initial Trial Results after 4 Years." *Science* 270

(October 20, 1995): 475–480. Blaese and his colleagues summarize the DeSilva trial and discuss some of the issues that need to be resolved before gene therapy becomes a routine medical procedure.

Boudreau, Ryan, et al. "Nonallele-Specific Silencing of Mutant and Wild-Type Huntingtin Demonstrates Therapeutic Efficacy in Huntington's Disease Mice." *Molecular Therapy* 17 (2009): 1,053–1,063. In their latest paper, Beverly Davidson's group explores the possibility of using an RNA interference-based gene therapy to treat Huntington's disease.

Cavazzano-Calvo, Marina, and Alain Fischer. "Gene Therapy for Severe Combined Immunodeficiency: Are We There Yet?" *The Journal of Clinical Investigation* 117 (June 2007): 1,456–1,465. An interesting review article that summarizes the successes and failures of SCID-X1 gene therapy.

Church, George. "Genomes for All." *Scientific American* 294 (2006): 46–54. This article discusses fast and cheap DNA sequencers that could make it possible for everyone to have their genome sequenced, giving new meaning to personalized medicine.

Collins, Francis, Michael Morgan, and Aristides Patrinos. "The Human Genome Project: Lessons from Large-Scale Biology." *Science* 300 (2003): 286–290. Provides an overview of the many organizational problems that had to be overcome in order to complete the project.

Fretag, Svend, et al. "Phase I Trial of Replication-Competent Adenovirus-Mediated Suicide Gene Therapy Combined with IMRT for Prostate Cancer." *Molecular Therapy* 15 (May 2007): 1,016–1,023. Gene therapy is used to induce the destruction of prostate cancer cells.

Gong, Zhiyuan, et al. "Development of Transgenic Fish for Ornamental and Bioreactor by Strong Expression of Fluorescent Proteins in the Skeletal Muscle." *Biochemical and Biophysical*

Research Communications 308 (August 15, 2003): 58–63. Scientists have produced transgenic zebrafish that glow orange, green, red, and yellow.

Hacein-Bey-Abina, Salima, et al. "Insertional Oncogenesis in 4 Patients after Retrovirus-Mediated Gene Therapy of SCID-X1." *The Journal of Clinical Investigation* 118 (September 2008): 3,132–3,142. The Fischer team describes the conditions and treatment schedules for four patients who developed leukemia after receiving gene therapy.

Jacobson, Samuel, et al. "Identifying Photoreceptors in Blind Eyes Caused by *RPE65* Mutations: Prerequisite for Human Gene Therapy Success." *Proceedings of the National Academy of Science* 102 (2005): 6,177–6,182. An important paper that characterizes mutations in *RPE65*, a gene essential for the normal function of the human retina.

Kaplitt, Michael, et al. "Safety and Tolerability of Gene Therapy with an Adeno-Associated Virus (AAV) borne *GAD* Gene for Parkinson's Disease: An Open Label, Phase I Trial." *The Lancet* 369 (June 23, 2007): 2,097–2,105. The first time gene therapy has been used to boost the production of a neurotransmitter in order to alleviate some of the symptoms of PD.

Leary, Rebecca, et al. "Integrated Analysis of Homozygous Deletions, Focal Amplifications, and Sequence Alterations in Breast and Colorectal Cancers." *PNAS* 105 (October 21, 2008): 16,224–16,229. A team, led by Burt Vogelstein and Kenneth Kinzler, characterizes gene mutations associated with breast and colon cancer.

Morgan, Richard, et al. "Cancer Regression in Patients after Transfer of Genetically Engineered Lymphocytes." *Science* 314 (October 6, 2006): 126–129. Steven Rosenberg's team at NCI treat melanoma with gene therapy.

Nagahara, Alan, et al. "Neuroprotective Effects of Brain-Derived Neurotrophic Factor in Rodent and Primate Models of

Alzheimer's Disease." *Nature Medicine* 15 (2009): 331–337. Mark Tuszynski's group examines the potential of nerve growth factor as a therapy for AD in preparation for human clinical trials.

Rafnar, Thorunn, et al. "Sequence Variants at the *TERT-CLPTM1L* Locus Associate with Many Cancer Types." *Nature Genetics* 41 (January 18, 2009): 221–227. Kari Stefansson's team identifies a DNA region that is associated with the onset of 16 types of cancer.

Ratjen, Felix. "Cystic Fibrosis: Pathogenesis and Future Treatment Strategies." *Respiratory Care* 54 (May 2009): 595–605. The author reviews the many treatment strategies for cystic fibrosis, including recent attempts to use liposome-based gene therapy.

Sasaki, Erika, et al. "Generation of Transgenic Non-Human Primates with Germline Transmission." *Nature* 459 (May 28, 2009): 523–527. Japanese scientists have produced green-glowing transgenic monkeys by injecting embryos with a viral vector containing the gene for green fluorescent protein.

Villarreal, Luis. "Are Viruses Alive?" *Scientific American* 291 (2004): 101–105. A fascinating discussion of what it means to be a virus.

Wood, L. D., et al. "The Genomic Landscapes of Human Breast and Colorectal Cancers." *Science* 318 (November 16, 2007): 1,079–1,080. A team, led by Burt Vogelstein and Kenneth Kinzler, determines the number of gene mutations associated with breast and colon cancer. See the follow-up paper "Leary, Rebecca, et al." above.

ARTICLES ON THE INTERNET

Altman, Lawrence. "Three Win Nobel in Medicine for Gene Technology." *New York Times,* October 9, 2007. Available online. URL: http://www.nytimes.com/2007/10/09/science/09nobel. html?_r=1&scp=1&sq= 3+Win+Nobel+in+Medicine+for+ Gene+Technology&st=nyt. Accessed October 1, 2009. This report profiles two Americans and a Briton who won the Nobel prize for developing gene "knockout" technology.

Clarke, Toni. "Genzyme Bets on Gene Therapy as Others Steer Clear." *Reuters,* June 21, 2007. Available online. URL: http://www.reuters.com/article/health-SP/idUSN2135767920070621. Accessed October 1, 2009. The biotech company, Genzyme, is developing a gene therapy for Parkinson's disease.

Food and Drug Administration. "Cellular & Gene Therapy Products." Available online. URL: http://www.fda.gov/Biologics BloodVaccines/CellularGeneTherapyProducts/default.htm. Accessed October 1, 2009. Provides information regarding gene therapy clinical trials, compliance actions, and the gene therapy patient tracking system.

Gelsinger, Paul, and Adil Shamoo. "Eight Years after Jesse's Death, Are Human Research Subjects Any Safer?" *Hastings Center Report* 38, no. 2 (2008): 25–27. Available online. URL: http://www.thehastingscenter.org/Publications/HCR/Detail.aspx?id=82. Accessed July 10, 2009. This report chronicles the problems CIRCARE has had in trying to improve the safety of clinical trials.

Human Genome Project. "Gene Therapy." Available online. URL: http://www.ornl.gov/sci/techresources/Human_Genome/medicine/genetherapy.shtml. Accessed October 1, 2009. This article discusses gene therapy and recent developments in the field.

Luo, Ji, and Stephen Elledge. "Cancer: Deconstructing Oncogenesis." *Nature* 453 (2008): 995–996. Available online. URL: http://www.nature.com/nature/journal/v453/n7198/full/453995a.html. Accessed October 1, 2009. A news article that discusses the search for gene mutations that are responsible for cancer formation.

National Center for Biotechnology Information. "Genes and Disease." Available online. URL: http://www.ncbi.nlm.nih.gov/books/bv.fcgi?rid=gnd&ref=sidebar. Accessed October 1, 2009.

An online book that discusses genetic disorders and provides diagrams of each human chromosome showing the location of the relevant genes.

National Institutes of Health. "Stem Cell Information." Available online. URL: http://stemcells.nih.gov/index.asp. Accessed October 1, 2009. Covers both the scientific and political aspects of stem cell research.

SSKRP Attorneys at Law. "The Gelsinger Lawsuit." Available online. URL: http://www.sskrplaw.com/links/healthcare2.html. Accessed October 1, 2009. The details of the lawsuit, by the law firm that handled the case.

Weiss, Rick, and Deborah Nelson. "Penn Settles Gene Therapy Suit: University Pays Undisclosed Sum to Family of Teen Who Died." *Washington Post,* November 4, 2000. Available online. URL: http://www.washingtonpost.com/ac2/wp-dyn?pagename=article&node=&contentId=A11512-2000Nov3. Accessed October 1, 2009. Discusses the conclusion of the civil suit concerning Jesse Gelsinger's death.

Wren, Jonathan, et al. "Plant Virus Biodiversity and Ecology." *PLOS Biology* 4 (2006): 314–315. Available online. URL: http://biology.plosjournals.org/perlserv/?request=get-document&doi=10.1371/journal.pbio.0040080. Accessed October 1, 2009. This article discusses the number and types of viruses that infect terrestrial organisms.

WEB SITES

Department of Energy Human Genome Project. Available online. URL: http://genomics.energy.gov. Accessed October 1, 2009. Covers every aspect of the human genome project and current genome programs with extensive color illustrations.

Genetic Science Learning Center at the University of Utah. Available online. URL: http://learn.genetics.utah.edu/. Accessed on October 1, 2009. An excellent resource for beginning students.

This site contains information and illustrations covering basic cell biology, gene therapy, animal cloning, stem cells, and other new biology topics.

Google Video. Available online. URL: http://video.google.com/ videosearch?q=histology+tissue&emb=0&aq=3&oq=histology #q=gene+therapy&emb=0. Accessed October 1, 2009. This site contains many videos covering gene therapy, including discussions of the basic procedure and the results of some recent trials.

Journal of Gene Medicine. "Gene Therapy Clinical Trials Worldwide." Available online. URL: http://www.wiley.co.uk/gene therapy/clinical. Accessed October 1, 2009. A very comprehensive site that provides detailed information about gene therapy trials, including the types of vectors used and the gene being transferred. The user can also search a database by trial country, disease category, trial status, and several other parameters.

National Cancer Institute. Available online. URL: http://www. cancer.gov/. Accessed October 1, 2009. This site, established by the National Institutes of Health, covers basic cancer information and links to gene therapy clinical trials.

National Center for Biotechnology Information (NCBI). Available online. URL: http://www.ncbi.nlm.nih.gov. Accessed October 1, 2009. This is an excellent resource for anyone interested in biology. The NCBI provides access to GenBank (DNA sequences), literature databases (Medline and others), molecular databases, and topics dealing with genomic biology. With the literature database, for example, anyone can access Medline's 11,000,000 biomedical journal citations to research biomedical questions. Many of these links provide free access to full-length research papers.

National Health Museum Resource Center. Washington, D.C. Available online. URL: http://www.accessexcellence.org/RC/. Accessed October 1, 2009. Covers many areas of biological research, supplemented with extensive graphics and animations.

National Human Genome Research Institute (United States). Available online. URL: http://www.genome.gov/. Accessed October 1, 2009. The institute supports genetic and genomic research, including the ethical, legal, and social implications of genetics research.

National Institutes of Health (United States). Available online. URL: http://www.nih.gov. Accessed January 1, 2009. The NIH posts information on their Web site that covers a broad range of topics including general health information, stem cell biology, aging, cancer research, and much more.

Nature Publishing Group. Available online. URL: http://www.nature.com/nature/supplements/collections/humangenome/commentaries. Accessed October 1, 2009. The journal *Nature* has provided a comprehensive guide to the human genome. This site provides links to the definitive historical record for the sequences and analyses of human chromosomes, All papers, which are free for downloading, are based on the final draft produced by the Human Genome Project.

Sanger Institute (United Kingdom). Available online. URL: http://www.sanger.ac.uk. Accessed October 1, 2009. DNA sequencing center, named after Fred Sanger, inventor of the most commonly used method for sequencing DNA. The institute is also involved in projects that apply human DNA sequence data to find cures for cancer and other medical disorders.

United States Food and Drug Administration. Available online. URL: http://www.fda.gov/BiologicsBloodVaccines/default.htm. Accessed October 1, 2009. Provides extensive coverage of general health issues and regulations, including gene-based treatments and products.

Virology. Available online. URL: http://www.virology.net/garry favweb.html. Accessed October 1, 2009. This site provides extensive coverage of basic virology, with many pictures and links to additional resources.

# Index

Page numbers in *italic* indicate photos or illustrations.

argininosuccinate *91*
asparagine *10*
aspartic acid *10*
atherosclerosis 34–35
atoms 154–156
ATP. *See* adenosine triphosphate
autosomal recessive genetic defect 74
avian influenza *60*

B

bacteria. *See* prokaryotes
bacterial artificial chromosomes (BACs)
    12, 13
bacteriophage 3–5, *4*
bacteriophage lambda 178–179
baldness 119
basal cell 30, *31*
basal cell carcinoma 32
base-flippers 168
basophils *77*
Batshaw, Mark 89, 97, 98, 135
Belmont Report 121–125
beneficence 123
bilirubin 96–97
biotechnology. *See* recombinant DNA
    technology
bioterrorism 120
Blaese, Michael 72, 81, 82, 86, 130
blood clot
    in disseminated intravascular coagula-
        tion 97
    formation of 36–37, *37*
    functions of 36
blood transfusions 38
B lymphocytes *77*
    activated 78, 80
    function of 39, 75
    in severe combined immunodefi-
        ciency 72, 80
bone marrow transplant 40, 80, 81, 85
brain stem 42, *43*
brain tumors 22
Brca1 gene 27
Brca2 gene 27
breast cancer 27–28, *28*

breeders 2
budding, of viruses *66*
Burkitt's lymphoma 22

C

cancer. *See also* specific cancers
    gene mutations and 22–23
    gene therapy trials for 27–34,
        142–144
Caplan, Arthur 135
capsid
    of adenoviruses *53*, 54, *56*, 63, *64*
    definition of 20
    in endocytosis 61–63, *62*
    evolution of 60–61
    of HIV 54–56, 62–63
    of retroviruses 54–56, 62–63, *65*
    structure of 52–53, *53*
carbohydrates 161
carboxyl group 159, *160*, 161, 162
cardiovascular diseases 34–35
Cdkn2 gene 33–34
cDNA. *See* complimentary DNA
cell(s) 154–176, *155*
    basic functions of 166–176
    communication of 175–176
    definition of 154
    evolution of 156
    macromolecules of 162–165, *163*
    molecules of 159–162, *160*
    structure of 156–159, *157*
cell cycle 170–176, *171*
cell membrane 61, *62*, *157*
cellulose 161
Center for Biologics Evaluation and
    Research (CBER) 131–132
central nervous system (CNS)
    ammonia levels and 92
    components of 42, *43*
    disorders of 42–47, 150–153
centromere 173
centrosome *157*
cerebellum 42, *43*
cerebral atrophy *45*
cerebral cortex 42

DNA (deoxyribonucleic acid). *See also*
      transcription; translation
   cloning 176–178, *177*
   complimentary 179, 182, 183
   discovery of 3–5, *4*
   function advantage over RNA 54
   integration of 103–105, *104*
   labeling cloned 179–180
   maintenance of 167–168
   mutations altering 21–23
   noncoding 14, *17*, 18–19
   replication of 166–167, 173, 180, 184
   structure of 5, *6, 7, 8*, 162, *163*, 165
   transposable genetic elements of 15,
      18–20
DNA damage checkpoints 172–173
DNA libraries *177*, 178–179
DNA ligase 176, 178
DNA polymerase 166–167, 180, 181,
   184
DNA sequencing *177*
   Sanger method of 7, 11, 181–182
   shotgun method of *12*, 13
DNA viruses 53, *53*, 54, *55, 56*, 63, *64*
double helix 5, *6, 7, 8*, 165
Duchene muscular dystrophy (DMD)
   41–42
dystrophin 41

E

Ebola-HIV viral hybrid 70
Ebola virus *69*
*Eco*RI (restriction enzyme) 178
electron transport chain. *See* respiratory
   chain
endocytosis 61–63, *62*
endoplasmic reticulum (ER) *157*, 159
Energy, Department of 11
Env gene 57
eosinophils *77, 78*
epidermis 30, *31*
ethical issues of gene therapy 121–129
eukaryotes
   cell membranes of 61, *62, 157*
   evolution of 71, 156

gene mutations in 20
gene organization in 16–18, *17*
genome of *17*, 19–20, 156, 158
proteins in 164
structure of 156–159, *157*
transposable genetic elements of
   18–20
European Agency for the Evaluation of
   Medicinal Products (EMEA) 140
evolutionary change
   gene mutations and 20–21
   jumping genes and 18–19, 71
exocytosis 63, *65*
exons 16–18, *17*
Experiments with Plant Hybrids (Mendel)
   3
eye
   color of 119
   properties of 47–49, *48*

F

F8 gene 38
F9 gene 38
fatty acids *160*, 161–162, 165
fibrin 37, *37*
fibrinogen 37, *37*
Filoviridae *69*
Fischer, Alain 102, 147
Fischer trial 102, 103, 105, 147–150
fluorescent in situ hybridization (FISH)
   183–184
Food and Drug Administration (FDA)
   on AD-vector gene therapy 98
   clinical trial applications made to 83
   drugs recalled by 84–85
   fraud on 137–138
   Gelsinger trial investigated by 101
   guidelines enforced by 124–125,
      126–127
   mission of 131
   regulation of gene therapy by xv, 101,
      130, 131–133
   on retroviral vectors 149
fovea 47, 49
Franklin, Rosalind 6

G

G$_0$ (phase in cell cycle) 171–172

G4 (bacteriophage) 11

GAD. *See* glutamic acid decarboxylase

Gag gene 57

gamma butyric acid (GABA) 152

ganglion cells (in retina) *48, 49*

Gap 1 170–172, *171*

Gap 2 170–172, *171*

gel electrophoresis *177,* 180–181, 182, 183

Gelsinger, Jesse xv, 90, *90,* 96–100

Gelsinger, John 135

Gelsinger, Paul 96, 97, 101, 135, 138, 140

Gelsinger trial 96–100, 105–106

    background of 89–90

    civil lawsuit after 135–140

    impact of 90, 100–101, 124, 133, 135, 146

    investigation of 98–100, 111, 125–126, 138–139

gene(s)

    definition of 2

    discovery of 2–5

    jumping. *See* jumping genes

    nomenclature of 185–186

    organization of 15–18, 19–20

    origins of 15

    overlapping 57

gene-corrected T lymphocytes 85–86

gene expression 168–169, *177,* 182–185

gene mutations 20–23. *See also* point mutations

    beneficial 20

    DNA altered by 21–23

    and evolutionary change 20–21

    lethal 21

    rate of 20, 21

generation time 172

gene swapping 15

gene therapy

    bizarre 119–120

    cosmetic 118–119, 128–129

    critics of xv, 88

    dangers of xv, xvi, 67, 68

    definition of 133

    diseases as candidates for xv, 25–50, 142–153. *See also* specific diseases

    domestic regulation of xv, 101, 130, 131–135

    efficiency of 108

    ethical issues of 121–129

    future prospects of 102–120

    germ line altered by 127–129

    goal of xiv

    immune system in xvi, 80, 106, 108–111

    improving safety of 102–112

    international regulation of xv, 140–141

    legal issues of 111, 130–141

    natural 15

    physiological 113–118, 127–128

    potential of xvi

    public access to information about 101

    transposable genome and 19–20

    viruses in xvi, 51–52, 66–70. *See also* specific viruses

Gene Therapy Advisory Committee (GTAC) xv, 140–141

genetic code 6–7, *9, 10*

genetic disorders. *See also* specific disorders

    as candidates for gene therapy xv, 25–50, 142–153

    monogenic 25, 41

    polygenic 25–26, 45

gene vehicle. *See* vector (viral)

genome

    definition of 2

    discovery of 5–6

    eukaryotic *17,* 19–20, 156, 158

    human. *See* human genome

    prokaryotic 156

    size of *14*

    transposable genetic elements of 15, 18–20

    viral. *See* viral genome

major histocompatibility complex (MHC)
  79
MAO. *See* monoamine oxidase
MAO gene 15
MART-1 antigen 143
maturation promoting factor (MPF) 172
Mc1r gene 34
McClintock, Barbara 18, *19*
Mda-7/IL-24 gene 144
meiosis 170, 174–175
meiosis I 174, 175
meiosis II 174, 175
melanin 30, 33
Melanocortin-1 receptor (Mc1r) gene 34
melanocytes 30, *31*, 32
melanoma 32, *33*, 143–144
membrane hybridization 183
Mendel, Gregor 2–3, *3*, 5
messenger ribonucleic acid (mRNA)
    in eukaryote genes *17*, 18
    location of 183
    in prokaryote genes 15–16, *16*
    role of 7, 158
    in transcription *9, 17*, 168
    in translation *9, 17*, 105, 151, 168
metaphase 173
metaphase plate 173
methionine *10*, 169
microtubules *157*
Milstein, Alan 138
mimivirus 71
missing tooth 167, 168
mitochondria
    ATP production by 113, *114*,
        115–116, *157*, 159, 169
    transmission electron micrograph
        of *115*
mitosis 170, 173–174
Mlh1 gene 29
mobile genetic elements (transposable
    elements) 15, 18–20
molecules *155*
    of cell 159–162, *160*
    definition of 156
    evolution of 156

hydrophilic 161
hydrophobic 161–162
monoamine oxidase (MAO) 15
monoamines 15
monocytes 75, *77*
monogenic disorders 25, 41
monosaccharides 161, *163*, 165
MPF. *See* maturation promoting factor
M phase 170–172, *171*
MRI. *See* magnetic resonance imaging
Msh2 gene 29
multicellular organisms *155*, 156
murine leukemia virus (MLV) 67, 85,
    103
muscular dystrophy 41–42
mutagenesis, insertional 19, 149–150
mutations. *See* gene mutations; point
    mutations
Myc gene 185–186
Myc protein 22, 185–186
Myc proto-oncogene 22
myelogenous leukemia 23

N

NADH dehydrogenase 113–115, *114*,
    169, 170
National Cancer Institute (NCI) 34, 143
National Institutes of Health (NIH) *73*
    ADA deficiency trial at 72, 81
    on AD-vector gene therapy 90, 98
    clinical trial applications made to 83
    Gelsinger trial investigated by
        98–100, 101, 111
    gene therapy trials funded by 131,
        132, 134–135
    guidelines enforced by 101, 124–125,
        126–127
    mission of 133–134
    regulation of gene therapy by xv, 101,
        133–135
    on retroviral vectors 149
    on risk assessment 111
National Research Act (1975) 122
National Research Council (NRC) 11

natural killer (NK) cells *77*
    activated 78–80
    in disseminated intravascular
        coagulation 97
    function of 75
    gene therapy vectors attacked by 108
    immunosuppressants and 108
Nature (journal) 5
Necker Hospital 147
NeoR gene 82
nerve growth factor (NGF) 150, 152
neurological disorders 42–47, 150–153
neutrophils *77*
nicotinamide adenine dinucleotide
    (NAD) 113, 115, 170
nitrogen fixation 93
noncoding DNA 14, *17,* 18–19
nuclear envelope 174
nuclear localization sequence (NLS)
    21–22, 147
nucleotides
    codons for *9, 10*
    damage to 167–168
    in DNA replication 166–167, 180
    radioactive 180
    structure of *160,* 162
nucleus 156, *157,* 158
Nuremberg code of ethics 121

O

Office of Biotechnology Activities (OBA)
    132, 134
Office of Human Subjects Research 132
oligosaccharides 165
opsin *48,* 49
ornithine transcarbamylase (OTC) 22,
    40–41, *91,* 91–92
ornithine transcarbamylase (OTC)
    deficiency 40–41
    gene involved in 41, 93–94
    gene therapy trials for 41, 89–90,
        94–100
    partial 94
    treatment of 41

Orthomyxoviridae *60*
ovarian cancer 27
oxygen, in respiratory chain 115,
    116–117

P

P16 gene 33, 34
Parkinson, James 46
Parkinson's disease 46, 152–153
patient advocate 124, 135
PCR. *See* polymerase chain reaction
PEG. *See* polyethylene glycol
PEG-ADA 80, 81, 85
peroxisome *157,* 159
phage 3–5, *4*
phagocytosis 75, 78, *79*
Phase I clinical trials 81, 82–84
Phase II clinical trials 84
Phase III clinical trials 84
Phase IV clinical trials 84–85
phenylalanine *10,* 21, 36
Philadelphia chromosome 23, *23*
phosphates *160,* 161, 162
phospholipids *163,* 165. *See also* lipid
    vectors
photoreceptors 47–49, *48*
PHS. *See* Public Health Service
physiological gene therapy 113–118,
    127–128
pigmented epithelium *48,* 49
pituitary gland *43*
plasmids 58–61, 176–178
point mutations 21–22
    in Alzheimer's disease 45
    in breast cancer 27
    in colon cancer 29
    in cystic fibrosis 22, 35–36
    in hemophilia 38
    in Huntington's disease 47
    in Leber congenital amaurosis 47,
        50
    in muscular dystrophy 41
    in OTC deficiency 92–93
    in Parkinson's disease 46